After reading P
like I found a fi
mission. Many
between entrep
the beauty that
middle of the book leads to honest reflection. This book may be about part-time work, but it is about a full-time journey. — **Rev. Carl D. Johnson, Founder of Praxis and Pillar and Storehouse Grocers**

Benesh and Littleton give part-time ministry the honor and credibility it deserves. As the church in the United States continues a journey of reimagination, *Part-Time Pastoring* adds a needed voice to that conversation. Kingdom entrepreneurs will be challenged to think outside of the traditional box of pastoring. **— Doug Foltz, Senior Director of Project Development, Stadia**

In the age of COVID shutdowns, celebrity Christian moral failures and deconstructions no one knows what the institutional church is going to look like going forward. The next phase of church will likely be small groups of serious Christians figuring out how to build communities for groups of hurting people without a lot of money. This may mean the twilight of the "professional" clergy. Church leaders will still need to be knowledgeable and serious about godliness, but "real" will outpace "professional." This book is about the reality of church planting in a community as a community. The leaders aren't perfect. They fail sometimes but they persist. If you wonder if God might be calling you to serve in small places in big ways, you will definitely learn something from their stories. **— Paul VanderKlay, YouTuber and Pastor of Living Stones CRC in Sacramento, CA**

Part-Time Pastoring is an honest look at the benefits and pitfalls of bivocational ministry. It will get you thinking about how to integrate your faith and work as you lead God's people to live out that reality themselves. **— Caleb Melton, Pastor of The Table Charleston**

i

I read everything that Sean writes. He's a prophetic voice to the church planting world. A missionary at heart, Sean keeps ministry real, low-to-the-ground, and sacrificial. This book he co-wrote with Andy Littleton is for those who fear losing their full-time ministry gig, because it unveils the mystery that many of us have fathomed … that it's actually better on the other side of the bi-vocational fence. It's also for those who are champing at the bit to venture out, but lack the practical steps and know-how. *Part-Time Pastoring* provides both. **— Peyton Jones, Author of Church Plantology: The Art and Science of Planting Churches and Host of the Church Planter Podcast**

If there's one thing the pandemic season of 2020 has shown us—it's this: the 20th century patterns of church and culture—the old normal—are being replaced rapidly with a still emerging new normal. History is speeding up. The inherited 20th century patterns of doing church and being on Jesus' mission decreasingly resonate with the people we are called to engage. And yet culture remains curious—even fascinated—with Jesus of Nazareth.

This new Jesus-centered movement is emerging at the edges and margins of the Church. These called leaders often feel like misfits in the traditional organized Church—and they are increasingly called to hard and overlooked people and places. The good news is—as the 20th century wave has come ashore—another wave is forming. A series of waves actually.

This book you hold in your hands—or on your preferred mobile device—points us to a compelling new normal for those called to the apostolic edge. It tells the story of new patterns and a new normal. Andy Littleton and Sean Benesh are sharing a story we can easily find ourselves in going forward. Welcome to the next wave! **— Daniel Serdahl, Cultural architect & futurist | newlife.tv and PNW Catalyst | Stadia**

ANDY LITTLETON

PART-TIME PASTORING

SEAN BENESH

Part-Time Pastoring: Leading God's People by Integrating Faith and Work

Published by Intrepid. www.intrepidmissions.com

The mission of Intrepid is to elevate marginalized communities and people through training church planters, pastors, and missionaries to start social enterprises to sustain themselves long-term so they can seek the betterment of these overlooked and neglected places and people as they start new churches, businesses, and non-profits.

Intrepid
2034 NE 40th Ave. #414
Portland, OR 97212

Manufactured in the United States of America.

ISBN: 978-0-578-24147-0

Contents

PART-TIME

FOREWORD

BY ROD HUGEN

PASTORING

There are people in the kingdom of God that I greatly admire. My heroes aren't necessarily the famous pastors and church leaders who write the books and speak at the conferences and build the megachurches. I appreciate them, of course, but I don't hold them out as heroes. I greatly admire the gifted theologians and the brilliant Biblical scholars who help shape our views of God, but they aren't really my heroes, either.

While I think all missionaries and pastors are deserving of honor as Scripture defines it, my true heroes are the unsung pastors who somehow manage to work two- or three-day jobs while tending to their families and planting and building churches. Many of us come home, tired from our nine-to-five jobs, but these folks do that same thing, grab a quick dinner, and then head off to write a sermon or attend a church meeting or lead a Bible study or visit the sick while the rest of us turn on Netflix and call it a night. Their lives are busy and exhausting and, in the midst of all the chaos, they build the church and push forward the Kingdom of God. That seems heroic to me.

This book is about bi-vocational pastors and, I suspect, an indictment of the North American church that bi-vocationalism for pastors even exists. Paul contends that those who proclaim the gospel should get their living from the gospel. He personally chooses to make a living as a tent maker, but defends the practice of providing for the care of the elders who care for the flock. He actually declares them worthy of double honor—the honor of their office and honoraria. Respect and a salary. It seems we live in a time where Paul's injunction regarding this is ignored by Christians. That is sad to me.

Enid, my next-door neighbor for many years, was a wonderfully religious Jew who loved to tell me about the practices of her faith. She knew I was a pastor and worried that we might be poor. "There is an old joke we like to tell the rabbi," she would laugh, "it goes like this: 'Our rabbi would probably starve to death, but for the fact that he fasts two days a week.'" She told me that joke many times and we would always get a good laugh.

Despite not wanting me to talk about the Messiah having come, she would send a small check to my church regularly to help make sure I was properly supported. It was always for exactly $28. She explained that seven was the number of blessing and that fourteen was the number of double blessing. Twenty-one was obviously the number of triple blessing and, she went on to explain, twenty-eight was the number declaring countless blessings. It was a beautiful gift, both because it revealed her generous heart, but also because it honored one of the "rabbis" in her life.

In the Old Testament, one of the twelve tribes of Israel, the Levites, were set apart to serve God and their needs were to be provided for by the other eleven tribes. That simply meant that eleven people were called on collectively to provide support for themselves and one other person. Even a simple tithe of ten percent would mean that the Levites lived at the same economic level as the rest of the Israelites.

I know it is simplistic, but if there are eleven households in a church there is no reason a full-time pastor shouldn't be cared for at the average rate of the other eleven households. If we choose not to bring the legalities of the Old Testament system forward into the New Testament, the new age that ushers in Christ's coming and the radical love and generosity he pushes us toward, then providing for the care of a pastor should not be at all difficult, regardless of whether the pastor fasts or not.

Unless, of course, we are ungrateful or selfish or modern pastors who simply aren't worthy of their hire. Perhaps, like the sons of Eli, many pastors don't care about the people and are out to get the choice cuts of meat for themselves, to live leisurely, and take the best for themselves. The call to pastors is to love their people and the call to the people is to honor their pastors.

Being forced into bi-vocationalism smacks of a problem that ought to be addressed. Either pastors are at fault or congregations are. Notwithstanding all that, in our North American culture, it seems tithing and generous giving are not being lived out, which leaves pastors vulnerable and requires them to find alternative ways to provide for themselves and their families. In our setting, for the gospel to perpetuate, we need pastors, church pastors, and leaders willing to live bi-vocationally. There are inherent problems with that reality. I'll enumerate a few.

First, it requires that a pastor have a marketable skill that allows them to thrive in the "part-time" economy. Fixing coffee at Starbucks isn't going to provide the kind of income necessary to feed a family. Doing "temp work" anywhere may provide a little income at Christmas, but none of the normal benefits like health insurance or pension plans. Before plunging in to being a bi-vocational pastor, one needs to evaluate just how lucrative the other job really is. It may require more education or training or creativity to find a marketable skill one can utilize.

Second, pastors will need to determine which job is first. When I moved to Tucson to plant a church, I was initially able to maintain some of my accounting clients back in Phoenix, but I couldn't maintain the work load for long with any sort of integrity. In that case, I had control of my work product and could find flexible hours in which to do the work but it still required a significant time commitment which robbed the church of my energy and focus.

Later when I worked part-time as a counselor for Teen Challenge, I made it clear that planting the Village Church was my priority and that Teen Challenge would be a secondary pursuit. They hired me with those priorities clearly laid out. Even though clearly stated upfront, there were significant disagreements and disappointments as we sorted out those priorities in real time. When I was selected to be a delegate to the two-week-long denominational Synod, the management of Teen Challenge had to scramble to find a substitute to do my work. They had several fundraising events each year that required "all hands on deck" and I would have to beg off to do things for the church community instead, which created jealousy and envy.

There was a consistent balancing act to accommodate the two jobs. A church planter friend got a part-time job working at Costco through the Christmas rush where he was required to keep certain fixed hours that precluded him being able to do anything church-related. Finding work that melds well with serving as a pastor can be an overwhelming and stressful task.

Third, it is easy to fail to honor the commitment to spouse, family, and friends when one is required to be bi-vocational. So often the family gets the dregs of the day instead of the best hours. The clock and calendar demand attention and a family game night or a Saturday date with your spouse gets short shrift. It's usually easier to make the family subservient to the demands of the church or the second job. Church planters and pastors are already easily tempted to sacrifice marriage and family, and having the voice of a second employer making demands exacerbates the problem. It takes both the ability and a firm commitment to saying no to be able to set clear boundaries to manage the various demands on the pastor's time.

Fourth, I suspect the commandment most often broken by pastors is the command to keep the Sabbath day holy. Setting apart time for an entire day to rest and pursue a relationship with God is not just an opportunity, but a command equal to not murdering your boss or sleeping with your neighbor's spouse. So many pastors, who wouldn't think to steal or tell a lie, blithely ignore the expectations of the fourth commandment.

The demands of a complex schedule make Sabbath rest difficult to engage even though it is the obligation of the individual to make it happen. Oddly, when we most need the re-creation that Sabbath provides, it can also be the time when we most resist its beauty, thinking we just don't have time for it. Just as it is easy to rob our spouses and families of our presence in stressful times, so it becomes easy to ignore our need for intimacy with the Father when we look instead for more space to engage our work schedules.

There are benefits to being bi-vocational, of course. The first and foremost being that it steeps the pastor in the culture. It takes the pastor out of the world of academia and out into the streets. Sermons become filled with real-world illustrations and examples that are personally experienced rather than imagined or stolen from other sources when you have a "day job." I've encouraged church planters who are fully funded to find part-time employment for precisely that reason.

I'm a second-career pastor so it might seem unnecessary to re-engage, but culture changes dramatically and the world is never static. Being in the world and being an exegete of culture is crucial to grounded ministry. I was the chief financial officer of a large auto parts corporation before becoming a pastor, followed by stints as a business consultant and entrepreneur, and have had numerous opportunities to not only speak into the lives of business people, but to be able to understand the things they regularly face. My time as a counselor at Teen Challenge not only allowed me to speak truth to addiction issues, but more importantly helped me become much better educated in addiction realities and better able to pastor a church. Cultural awareness is a sweet gift to pastors.

Another benefit is the inherent change of scenery that a second job permits. Shaking up routines can ignite creativity and innovation that carries over into ministry. When we are stuck in routines, the world begins to close in. That can hurt a church. When I teach people to become disciplers, I often urge them to change their routines. Go to a different hair stylist, shop at a different grocery store, find a new coffee shop, or take up a new hobby. In changing our routines, we meet new people and God invites us into the lives of new people. A second job is an opportunity to re-create and be newly engaged.

Bi-vocational pastors are my heroes because I know how difficult the role of the pastor is. I know the pain of sitting at the bedside of a dying parishioner. I know the struggle of writing a sermon each week. I know the criticisms and arguments and slander that can kill a pastor's heart. I know the calls that come at two o'clock in the morning. I know the drudgery of routines that sap the soul. I know the demands of the world and the expectations of others. I know the power of the call of God on your life that doesn't let you run away. And I know the beauty of it all as the Kingdom grows and God comes close.

Sean and Andy are my heroes. They both serve the kingdom of God bi-vocationally. I like to imagine the delight that God takes in them. I pray that they know in the deepest places that he sings over them. I hope they know that they are treasured and loved and that their sacrifices do not go unnoticed. I long for them to know the beauty of Hebrews 6:10, "God is not unjust; he will not forget your work and the love you have shown him as you have helped his people and continue to help them."

May God use these men, and others like them, to grow his kingdom.

Rod Hugen
Pastor, The Village Community, Tucson, AZ
Tucson Cluster Leader, Classis AZ of the Christian Reformed Church in North America

PART-TIME

INTRODUCTION

WHY THIS CONVERSATION MATTERS

PASTORING

A debate began to build up steam. How long should we pastors spend preparing our sermons? Some of the guys in my pastor's group said twenty hours. A couple leaned toward thirty. One guy spoke up saying his school taught him to spend no less than forty. Another said that was "demonic." Then a guy said … "Well, I probably spend about ten to fifteen." You could tell he felt a little bad about it. Another guy pitched in, "Yeah, me too." A friend of mine, who later confessed to inflating his number, said he was in the same boat.

I looked around the table and noticed one defining factor. All the guys that spent less time on sermon prep were wearing hats (literally). All those guys had come to this pastors group from a job-site of some kind. They'd come from some form of work in which having nicely combed hair and a tucked in button-up wasn't an option. All these guys were part-time pastors. I, too, was wearing a hat.

When you wear multiple hats (See what I did there?), you have to adjust. When you split your time in ministry, your ministry is different. Different can be very good. Different, though, can feel very unacceptable or out of place. Is being part-time, or bi-vocational, or co-vocational (as some now call it) in ministry good? Is it an acceptable option? Is it a preferable option?

I had to speak up in that meeting. I threw out my opinion that the mid-size church is dying off. We'll likely have megachurches and little churches. Our church world will likely go the way of business. The big online powerhouses will stick around for some time, and those who reject the powerhouses will look for the boutiques. But, the era of mid-size, somewhat expensive to run, five-to-ten staff member churches that get funded by their donors or denominations, is ending.

Most of us around the table were living in the last era, in which churches, like ours, will offer us full-time jobs. Already, several didn't. Those that did would have been better served spending half of what it cost them to pay a full-time pastor on administration or outreach. I predicted the days of mid-size churches with full-time pastors may be over in twenty years. My friend from a large denomination disagreed. He thinks we'll chug on like this for another hundred, but then ... yes ... he agreed things will dramatically change.

Whatever the case, Christianity is declining in the West. We are already post-Christian. There are fewer Christians out in our neighborhoods already. Many adults in my city know very little about Christianity, and reject the little they know. The committed Christians don't give as much as they should. Many of them have been burned by it or just don't see its value. Something will have to change.

The fact is that if we feel truly called to "shepherd God's flock," most of us will have to do it without a lot of money. We'll either have to live extremely simple lives, or work another job … and often we'll have to do some combination of the two. This reality will become a major portion of discerning our call. Will I do this, if it pays me nothing at all?

What does that mean for the length of time we prepare a sermon? Well, it's hard to say, but it definitely changes your answer. There's a reason the guys wearing hats gave their sermons less time. It's not because they don't care or because they don't think deeply. Part-time pastors have to craft sermons in their minds as they do another job. They have to see the patterns in their work world, and wonder how the words of their text might land with their parishioners in their respective jobs. They have to process the background of a text through an audio book as they make deliveries. They have to learn what people believe these days as they steam milk from across the bar at the coffee shop.

Part-time pastoring you see, is different. It's different, but it can be very good. It will be what makes boutique ministries, and probably even mid-size churches, possible in the coming decades. It will be what connects ministry leaders to the people whom they want to reach but will never otherwise meet. But, it will require a different set of strategies.

Sean and I wrote this book because we have lived the part-time life for a while, and realized that we were blazing trails. We wrote this book because we wish somebody would have sat us down and worked out the benefits and pitfalls with us a long time ago. We wrote this book because we wanted to encourage you to consider this bi-vocational life, but also come at it with eyes wide open.

This book is by no means a "manual." This type of work is too varied and, we assume … if you're interested in the topic, you only have so much available time. We hope this little book gets you thinking and gives you some direction. If we achieve that, we'll be grateful!

Hoping to hear your story someday!

Andy Littleton
Tucson, AZ
March 2020

PART-TIME

CHAPTER 1

OUR JOURNEYS

PASTORING

Part-time pastoring was and is born out of *our* stories. They are just that, our stories. These stories are deeply personal. More than that, as you will discover, they were born out of figuring things out on the fly rather than a predetermined path. In other words, neither of us set out on a ministry trajectory with the goal of being bi-vocational. But for a variety of reasons, that is where we both ended up. As you will read and discover in this chapter and throughout the book, it is a reality and a lifestyle, that though not neat and tidy, we not only embrace, but love deeply.

Andy's Story

When I was eighteen I became a ministry leader. I began to volunteer lead within the youth ministry I'd just graduated from. I met with a younger kid as his prayer partner. I helped chaperone middle-school kids at the out-of-state youth convention. To pay my new rent obligation I worked at the local car audio shop selling and installing stuff like subwoofers and XM radios. I assumed I'd be a car audio guy for life.

Then I attended a youth convention as a leader. One of the speakers got my attention. He emphatically urged some of the young people to consider devoting their entire lives to ministry. I remember him saying that we were all called to live for Jesus, but that God was calling some of us to do it full-time. I'd been watching the lives of the owners and my co-workers at the car audio shop throughout the year and was becoming increasingly disillusioned. The drive to make money wasn't cutting it for me. I wanted to talk to the people about the reasons they were blowing their whole paychecks on upgraded amps and speakers. I wanted to talk to my co-workers about their problems in life and the reasons they were so unhappy. The conference speaker struck a chord. I wanted to live for more ... and I wanted to do it full-time.

When I got home I announced to my small church family that I felt called to full-time ministry and that I wanted to start as soon as possible. Surprisingly, they offered me a job. My tasks included trimming the trees, logging attendance, playing the bongos, visiting the sick and hospitalized, and doing the announcements. I was officially in full-time ministry. I figured I'd stay on that train the rest of my life.

Well ... life's a little more complicated than that. God, I suppose, is a little more thorough than that. That job lasted about a year. When the church hired a new pastor, they couldn't afford me anymore. From there I wove in and out of ministry and retail work hybrids. The goal I continued to strive for was full-time ministry, but it kept slipping through my fingers. The closest I came was a six-year stint as a middle school director at a large church in Tucson, my home city.

I almost lost that job when my marriage fell apart. I found myself living as a single dad with an oversized mortgage. I stepped away from the ministry position, but the church refused to let me go officially. They paid me my full salary to remodel a donated house and get a lot of care and counseling. After a while, they gradually brought me back on staff. From then on, I had a reputation as a "Mr. Fix It." Thank God! I needed the extra money. People from the church began to hire me to do handyman work on the side on a fairly regular basis.

After a couple more years at that church, I started to realize that I was moving toward working with the parents more than the kids in my youth ministry. I had a great team around me that could carry the ministry forward, so I began to pursue a position in which I could learn to preach and lead the church as a whole. The internship I found, that interested me most, could offer ten paid hours a week. I knew what to do. I would just start advertising my handyman skills to the folks I'd worked for at church and see if they'd share my contact info. I'd do that until I finished my internship, and then I'd get back to being full-time.

The trouble is … that my plan worked. I got handyman gigs, and a decent amount of them. A coffee shop hired me to project-manage the opening of their new store after I successfully tackled a few other projects for them. I hired a friend to help make mesquite wood countertops for the coffee shop, and they turned out really nice. All of a sudden, I couldn't handle the workload and my friend ended up taking most of it on, which meant I had an employee. A job of ours got published and we had a budding reputation. After that we became known as a high-end custom furniture company. It's all kind of crazy to me.

My other plan also "worked." I started a small church alongside the small group I led during my internship. We were small and simple, but had all the responsibilities a church has. I remember my first funeral … a high-ranking military officer who wasn't a Christian, but was the grandfather of a young lady at our church. I had work to do all week. I had to preach on Sunday and finish up client projects. I also had to prepare to lead a family through a monumental and complicated moment in their lives. In the midst of it all, I got sick and lost my voice. I eked through the funeral ceremony and everything else I had to do. It was one of many times I struggled to manage my new and complex schedule.

A few years later we merged with another small church. These days we come across as fairly established. We worship regularly, people are gathering in one another's homes for prayer and Bible reading throughout the week, we have active elders and deacons, and we keep ourselves plenty occupied with ministry-esque activities. At first, I didn't get paid by the church because we started with eight people in a neighbor's backyard. Today I do get paid a modest amount, which I really appreciate. If I wanted to, I could easily give full-time energy to pastoring the church. But ... after all these years ... I've opted not to be in what most would call "full-time ministry."

The reason I've made this choice is not the money. In fact, at some points, running my small business has been a monetary drain. At one point I began to consider selling the business to someone more savvy and focused, but I decided not to completely disengage from it. The deciding factor in that decision was twofold. First of all, I love the business I've built with friends and I care about the people involved. Second, it's a huge part of my ministry. Through the business I meet a lot of people who don't know Jesus, and I have an extra level of connection with the people who work in my company. I've come to the conclusion that letting my "part-time" job go would actually diminish my calling as a minister of the gospel to my city.

The title of this book is a little deceiving. It represents the way I used to view work as opposed to ministry. These days I have come to believe that every Christian is a full-time minister. I have a specific skill set which includes me teaching and leading others more often. I have a sense of calling (the original meaning of vocation) from God to build his church. That calling, though, doesn't mean I don't generate income or work for any other entity than my local church. In fact, my work among the members of my community may actually be the way I most faithfully exercise my call. So I don't think I am a "part-time pastor." I think I shepherd people full-time ... sometimes in our church gatherings and sometimes at my wood shop, retail store, or in a community meeting. That discovery has come with time. I hope my journey will help illuminate yours.

Sean's Story

I gave my life to Christ right out of high school. It was a whirlwind experience. While I wasn't 100 percent sure what I wanted to do in life I had started the fall semester at a local community college as an art major. Art was a significant component of my life up until that point. All throughout high school, the only subject I cared about and was relatively decent at was related to art.

The plan was simple. Graduate from high school and head off to art school ... Chicago, Minneapolis, I hadn't locked that down yet. I was also an athlete. I remember being recruited by Boise State University to play football. One of my teammates' brothers coached there. When he was home visiting he came to one of our games. Honestly, I was too intimidated and insecure to ever reply. Boise was a long way from Iowa. Burdened by indecision and in a serious relationship with my girlfriend, I simply opted to enroll at the local community college. In the midst of it all, it was there that I came to faith in Christ. I had no idea what any of that meant.

The topics of calling and vocation are near and dear to my heart. It's something I teach on regularly in the university classroom and it's also the subject of a book I just had published. While I feel I'm now slowly learning the rhythms and contours of this conversation, almost thirty years ago it was a topic or subject I literally knew nothing about. All I knew was this ... before Christ my life was a dumpster fire. He rescued me. In response all I wanted to do was serve him and give my life to him. I didn't know anything about paid ministry and all of the different ways one could do that. (The rural church where I came to Christ was led by a pastor who worked full-time as a small-business owner.) I just said, "Lord, my life is yours. I give it all to you. I'll do whatever you tell me to do and go wherever you want me to go." That's it. That's all I knew.

During that first school year in community college taking art, art history, and other general classes, I kept thinking about my new life in Christ and my desire to "give it all to him." As people in my small church heard me say that they suggested that perhaps God was calling me into full-time ministry. Since I didn't know much of what that meant I simply assumed they were right.

Someone suggested I go to a Christian college. Since I wasn't in the arguing mood, I said, "Why not?" I began searching for these kinds of schools all over the Midwest. I visited a few and landed on one. By the following fall, I arrived on campus. I began my journey as a missions major and by the end of the first year switched to pastoral ministries. For me at that stage of my life, my calling was a mixture of higher education and discipleship. I was learning and growing in my new faith.

Since art was part of the "old me" and my unspectacular life before Christ, I basically set it aside. Besides, I was up to my ears studying Greek, theology, the Bible, and ministry. Art was not part of this new career pathway ... or so I thought, but I'm getting ahead of myself. Since there's too much ground to cover and too little space, I'll jump to where my life, ministry, and career went off the rails ...

Fast forward the story line ... I was on the typical ministry career path. In a whirlwind I graduated, got married, started seminary, and went on staff as a youth pastor in Arizona. Big move. While it was initially part-time, it didn't matter as I was in seminary. Sure, for a ten-month stretch I was a bank teller (and horrible at it). All through college I worked random jobs. I never had a disdain for non-ministry employment. But like Andy's story, I thought a life of ministry was meant to be a full-time gig, so that was what I was aiming for. Sure enough, I landed a full-time youth ministry role at a larger church in California. It was the opposite of part-time. It was probably more like two-to-three full-time roles all squeezed into one.

But, like most of those who start off at youth ministry, I realized that I was overworked, under-paid, and I had the worst times getting along with my senior pastors. I was always in trouble. From stern lectures in the senior pastor's office to getting yelled at via voicemail it was a miserable existence. Oh, the junior high, high school, and college students as well as my volunteers were amazing. Everything else, not so much.

Looking back, that artistic part of me was still alive and well. I simply didn't recognize it. It was also one of the reasons I kept getting in trouble. I would start programs and ministries and change things around. That never made either senior pastor happy at all.

By this time, I was full-throttle into full-time ministry. Running constantly on fumes, gone too much, and playing damage control at home. I thought God needed me. Luckily, my ineptitude as a youth pastor was revealed. The senior pastor gave me two options in light of declining youth ministry numbers: (1) resign now and they'll give me a good recommendation, or (2) get the youth group numbers back up to their historic highs within three months (even though they were already in decline by the time I showed up), if I fail, they'll fire me and not give me a good recommendation.

In the midst of this all, before any of this came up, I was already seriously considering church planting. We had even nailed down a place. So when I received this ultimatum, I chose to leave quietly and move down to Tucson to plant a church. If art and creativity weren't already bubbling up, they would soon burst open. It's like the storyline of a volcano. The pressure from molten magma builds up under the surface. As the pressure intensifies the cone grows until one day it erupts spilling lava everywhere. Moving to Tucson did that for me.

Church planting is the ultimate creative endeavor. You're literally creating something from nothing. While the process was invigorating, intense, and difficult it was what was happening outside of the ministry world that changed my life. I got a job.

I'm not a very good fundraiser. I wasn't back then when we set out to plant a church. While we had a decent baseline of funding, it wasn't enough to sustain us. By that time, I had an undergrad degree with a double major in Pastoral Ministries and Biblical Studies. I was working on a Master's degree in Church Planting and Church Growth. Also, all of my life post-college involved being on staff at two churches. So what kind of job could I get or do? What was I even qualified for?

To this day I'm convinced it was the sovereign hand of God that opened doors for me. I became a hiking and mountain biking guide. I had enough personal experience as well as a good fitness level to do both. Plus the schedule was favorable to church planting life. I'd be on the trail during most of the year by 6:00 AM (which meant getting to the shop by 5:15) and off the trail by 10 or 11 in the morning. After cleaning up and enjoying a meal of gourmet spa food, I'd head home and put on my church planting hat.

It was life-changing. Within months my life went from being on staff at a church surrounded by Christians to now church planting and working outside of the church world surrounded by those who don't identify with Christ. It was the first time I stepped outside the Christian bubble. Not only did I love it, but it fed this sense of calling, this missionary calling, that I had felt well up when I gave my life to Christ. I was living on the cutting edge of mission.

Since that day, I've found a life, career, and funding stream outside of the full-time ministry world. I've learned to no longer even differentiate between the two. Also, to be completely honest, in my paid part-time ministry world I am focused on training church planters, pastors, and missionaries which means it is filled with fellow followers of Jesus. But in my "non-ministry" world and jobs I am surrounded by people who don't necessarily identify with Christ. A lot of ministry takes place there. I spend half of my week in academia teaching and another portion of my week running the coffee-roasting company I started on a whim (which I had just sold during the end of writing this book. No worries, I started another business).

The biggest change that needed to happen was within me. I realized I wasn't crazy for living this way AND loving it. Andy's not crazy. You're not crazy for wanting to intentionally move in this direction. More than that, I was and am able to live out my calling more fully than if I had simply been in full-time paid ministry. You are too. Let's journey together ...

PART-TIME

CHAPTER 2

YOU'RE NOT CRAZY

PASTORING

A while back I (Andy) and my co-pastor Nick attended a micro-church brainstorming session in Colorado Springs at the beautiful Glen Eyrie Castle and Conference Center. Maybe it was the fact that small-church pastors were gathering in a castle on a breathtaking piece of premium property that is owned by one of the largest para-church ministries in the US, but I was feeling a little unsure of myself. Nick and I have been in ministry for a while, but our biggest accomplishments don't look like much compared to some of the pastors and churches we follow. We are very used to gatherings of pastors in which our way of doing church feels a bit "grassroots."

At the gathering, we discovered that most of the other leaders we met were sort of un-learning church. Many of them were coming out of larger and more established church systems. Many of them had become convinced that leading a church needed to look different, but hadn't received a lot of support in that direction. In fact, some of them reported that when they cast a vision of church that wasn't typical, that they had lost a lot of support.

A common thread that ran among these folks was the fact that they had begun to see that a life lived among unbelievers in their context was key. Most of them had found that their best road to real relationships had come through the "side hustle" that they had embraced to help them survive. Some of them had begun to realize that they actually didn't want to go back to full-time church work. Not only had they met people who didn't know Jesus in their other lines of work ... they had also discovered that they enjoyed what they got to do as much if not more than the church work they'd once learned.

One of the guys had come across a manufacturing company that had room in their warehouse for his church to meet. The owner of the company asked if he would be willing to serve in a coaching and counseling role with employees. Many of these employees were actually international refugees. All of a sudden, he found that his "side hustle" was bringing him face to face with the cultures we've considered to be on the "frontiers" of the mission field. He decided that this was one of his most important pastoral opportunities. He decided to shape his church around reaching and caring for the employees of the company. Many of the people of the church didn't understand and some of them left because of how this new emphasis changed the church. The pastor began to question if he was doing the right thing.

At the end of the weekend we all went around and shared one major takeaway. Nick and I both came away with new ideas and new connections, but the rest of the group had a nearly unanimous response. The pastor from the manufacturing company said it first ... "I don't feel crazy." In all the other gatherings of church leaders these folks had been to, their church's success was measured in "self-sufficiency." If the leader worked another job, it was a sign that something was wrong. In this gathering, though, all the leaders talked about and celebrated the ways God was working through their other jobs. Finally, we were around people who understood that we actually liked doing more than just one thing.

I had come into that weekend feeling a little unsure of myself. I'm used to talking to church leaders who seem to function like large company CEOs or professors at conferences. They usually just do pastoral work and seem to do it on a large scale of some sort. Conferences can oftentimes be places where pastors compare notes and church sizes. I'm kind of burned out on them, to be honest. But this conference left me feeling very different. We were in the company of like-minded folks.

Nick and I learned that the type of church leadership lives we'd been living for a decade was the type that many other pastors were longing to learn how to lead. We also walked away convinced that our experience would be valuable as large centralized churches continue to decline. For the gospel to reach as many people as possible, we'll need a multitude of churches. The amount of high-paying, large church positions are decreasing. The amount of people looking for a professional pastor is decreasing. Pastoring will increasingly become part-time. We can either do our other job grudgingly, or it can become part of our strategy. You're not crazy if you think that's a good idea … not crazy at all!

I'm Not Crazy … Another Layer

I (Sean) have been journaling daily since 1993. As a new Christian, I recall either reading about it or someone suggested it but that's when I started. I say daily, but there were stretches in the first number of years when it was more sporadic. However, over the last fifteen years I've settled on a good rhythm of journaling daily.

My bookshelf at home has all of my journals throughout this time. Until I settled on a routine, I was grabbing anything I could get my hands on to write in ... spiral bound notebooks and other variations large and small. Now I'm locked in on five-by-six leather-bound (or faux leather) journals. It works.

Since journaling is part of my daily Bible reading and prayer, I note which passages I'm reading, I transcribe the ones that jump out at me, and then what I'm praying about. I also reflect on what is going on in my life. Interestingly, there's a constant theme that has been evident throughout all of my journal entries over the past six-to-seven years ...

Am I crazy?

No, I don't mean that in a clinical sense. Over and over I'd make comments like ... "this juggling is maddening" ... "I feel torn" ... "I have divergent interests" ... "I feel pulled in so many different directions" ... and more. I felt like I was going crazy juggling everything between all of my side jobs and such. I have so many interests that at times I feel as if they're pulling at me and pulling me apart.

What was even more confusing was when these interests (and jobs) seemingly were at odds with each other. For example, there's the "city Sean" who's all-in on urban studies, urban history, urban ministry, and urban church planting. Then there's the "outdoors Sean" who leads a coffee roasting brand focused on mountain biking, trail-building, and even rural communities. These two parts of me have felt as if they were at war within me. Then there's the academic me, the creative me ... and all of a sudden, I felt like I was trying to lasso a tornado. Except the tornado was swirling within.

While there is much to be praised and applauded when it comes to part-time or bi-vocational or co-vocational ministry, it also comes with a warning label: it can be maddening. Rather than fight this inner tension and try to dispel it, over time I simply learned to live within the tension. It won't ever be neat and tidy. Nor does it have to be.

This morning, I felt the evidence of that tension. I began by working on a book I'm writing on an introduction to understanding cities, then I worked on social media for my coffee company (mountain biking, wilderness areas, etc.), and finally worked on promoting the Intrepid cohorts I lead for church planters wanting to launch startups. But I no longer think about the tension. I simply live within it.

Do you feel this way too? You're not crazy. Is your life full of tension? For sure. Do you … or will you feel torn and pulled in multiple directions? Yes. Is it worth it? One-hundred percent yes.

Breathe … You Got This

Hopefully our own stories normalize these feelings and to let you know that you're not alone. Sometimes we simply need permission to feel this way. The challenge is that in most of church planting legend and lore, as well as in local church ministry, bi-vocationalism isn't necessarily celebrated. It's almost a consolation prize for those who cannot land "real" ministry gigs or who are hoping their new church plant will grow to the point where they no longer have to work two jobs. But what if it turns out to be the preferred future or reality of pastoring?

You're not crazy to love your job outside of ministry. We've both discovered that we love, thrive, and are passionate about our lives and work that's not paid ministry. More often than not more ministry happens in those arenas than in our local churches. Especially for those of us with a heart and passion for evangelism, there's no better way to live this out. Embrace the crazy.

PART-TIME

CHAPTER 3

THE MANY PART-TIME PATHS

PASTORING

I (Andy) ignore a lot of emails. I especially tend to ignore emails from people I don't know, who want money. It's hard enough to keep up with supporting people in our church who are trying to get ministry done while working on a shoestring budget. On top of that … there's the vetting. It seems like ninety percent of the fund-seeking emails I get are fraudulent. Recently though, and I'm still not entirely sure why, I went for one of them.

We have our team meetings on Tuesday just after lunch, and that's right when the email popped up. It wasn't at all surprising. Someone was "searching for churches online" and found our website. He and his wife happened to be passing through town and were trying to "build a team" of people and churches to pray and of course … financially support them. Their goal was to "become full-time" in campus ministry in another state. I had never heard of this guy, and knew that I would be telling him no if I decided to respond at all.

I'm not sure what seemed different in this email. He did some things right, like adding a cell number, his photo, and links to a ministry website, but I don't think that's all there was to it. I sensed that God was giving me just a little extra nudge on this one. I felt like I should take the time to talk to this guy and see why he was reaching out to total strangers to ask for this support. I wondered if ministry had him a little beaten down. I also thought the chances of this being fraudulent were very low and, in case he didn't show up, I picked a coffee shop I was down to hang out at either way.

When I arrived, there he was as promised. He was great. He's a really nice guy, and the ministry he did sounded meaningful and necessary. He insisted on buying my coffee, which was a wonderful way to thank me for my time. He described how difficult a time he and his wife were having with raising enough support to keep their young little family afloat as they tried to focus on the students of the small college where they felt called to minister. He asked if our church could support them. I said no.

I could tell I stole the wind from his sails. I gave him our reasoning. At our church we try to give as much support as we can to members of our church who feel compelled to go and take the gospel elsewhere. The truth is that we don't give those folks nearly as much money or time as we wish we could. We also ask the people we send to find a way to work in order to partially support themselves as long as they're physically and legally able to. It's a way for us to test their dedication to the call, and to them it speaks volumes. It's also how all of our staff members at Mission function. We all work outside of our ministry roles in order to allow our church to be generous to its members and to the community. With these things in mind, shooting money his way at this time was out of the question.

I asked him if he was close to having enough support. He admitted that he really wasn't. At the moment he was working another job to make ends meet. I perked up. "Oh! What's your other skill?" He told me that he'd learned graphic design and was working for a company on the side. I said, "That's great!" He seemed a little confused. I pointed out that graphic design is super flexible. You typically can work remotely, and only have to meet deadlines as opposed to keeping office hours. On top of that, graphic design can get you into a relationship with all kinds of people you could potentially minister to! He seemed intrigued.

In no way did we solve all of his problems or craft a specific plan. We did though, explore the idea that graphic design could even be extremely strategic. It dawned on us that the college he worked in as a minister may need graphic design services, at least in one of its departments. If he found a job working within the school, offering a vital service, he may find that his relational reach was far greater than if he merely functioned within a disassociated campus ministry. Though we didn't exchange money, I felt that the conversation had become very valuable. We at least had the gears turning that could leverage his skillset to fund his life and ministry.

Now, I never would have manufactured the ideas we processed without meeting this guy and learning his specific story. This book will not manufacture the ideas for you. The truth is that each person needs to assess the skills they bring to the table, their personality, and their unique life situation. Your story will shape your ministry, and it will also shape the degree to which you might supplement or fully fund your ministry with the other work you do. There are many paths to part-time ministry … as many paths as there are people.

Finding Your Path

One of the greatest gifts you can give yourself in ministry is this … be yourself. Write your own story. Stop trying to emulate the paths of others. This is more than a cursory admonition against comparison, jealousy, and trying to fit into other people's shoes. Instead this is actually a deep work of the soul.

Park Palmer in his book *Let Your Life Speak* speaks into this as he references this tendency that we have for wearing other people's masks. He writes, "What a long time it can take to become the person one has always been! How often in the process we mask ourselves in faces that are not our own. How much dissolving and shaking of ego we must endure before we discover our deep identity—the true self within every human being that is the seed of authentic vocation."[1] Inevitably we all fall into this trap. We see "ministry success" or a certain pathway that others took before us and we assume that is the normative way to go. Not knowing any better, we follow suit only to realize and find out years later that all along we've been wearing the masks of others. Many of us simply didn't know any better.

Going into the ministry world we watch our predecessors and contemporaries and, again, simply assume that is the way to go. "Plant like

---

[1] Palmer, *Let Your Life Speak*, 9.

this." "Pastor or lead like this." "Preach or teach like this." Then there's a myriad of seminaries and conferences that only reinforce this. Sure enough, without realizing it we're on a trajectory that may be foreign and even at odds with how God has wired and gifted us. As a result, stepping away from this collective tradition makes us feel guilty as if we're doing something wrong.

That's why part-time pastoring or part-time church planting feels almost scandalous and even wrong. If we're really worth anything, then surely we'll do this full-time and of course have the support and finances to do so. I (Sean) can still hear the haunting refrain that goes something like "God's will done God's way will not lack God's resources." In other words, when we don't have enough money to do this full time then obviously we are doing something wrong. Somehow we've short-circuited this equation. We *must* be in sin or something.

Of course, this a very American notion. For the majority of the world, church planters, pastors, and missionaries work "normal" jobs and then do ministry "on the side." But here in the U.S. we've bought into the narrative that ministry *should* be done full-time and anything less is not what God intended. And so the storyline continues on and many church planters, pastors, and missionaries feel a deep-seated sense of guilt and even shame.

But what if it doesn't have to be that way?

What if part-time pastoring *is the plan?* There are endless joys, thrills, adventures, and opportunities to be found in creating multiple pathways that not only fund your ministry ... but ARE YOUR MINISTRY. That sounds like good news. Let's explore this more.

Over the past eighteen years of involvement in church planting and missions, most of the time I've been bi-vocational. Even when I was fortunate in a few seasons to have full-time work. either through a denomination or missions organization, I still maintained work outside of paid ministry. Whether that was as a professor or mountain biking guide I had to do something else or be sucked into the bubble known as ministry. I needed (and still do need) an outlet for exploration and creativity.

I've long since jettisoned even the notion that bi-vocational equals two jobs … paid ministry and paid work "outside" of ministry. Even though "bi" implies two, I'm currently in a season where my income stream comes from seven different places. Obviously not all are equal. Some comes from putting in twenty-plus hours a week and some may entail only five hours a month. Nonetheless, for me "bi-vocational" is oftentimes more than simply working two jobs.

Just to be clear, some of these income "buckets" include writing, graphic design, teaching, photography, teaching, ministry, and roasting coffee. One of my personal goals is to get up to ten income streams within the next year. Again, not all are equal. So why bother? Why not just have simply one job? One career? One place of employment?

In my early years out of college, I didn't know any better than working at one job and one job alone. That also seems to be somewhat the norm anyway. Or so I thought. What that also meant was that taking a new job meant I had to move across the country or to another state. That meant uprooting our lives, leaving friends, making new friends, getting acquainted with a new place and a new job. A few years later we'd do it again ... and again? One day I got tired of moving. So I stopped.

I was tired of chasing jobs or opportunities somewhere else only to realize that my boss or supervisor was a horrible micromanager focused solely on metrics. Or that the work environment was toxic and unhealthy. Oh, and I'm talking about work in the ministry world.

Since landing in Portland about a decade ago, I've had numerous opportunities to take a new job ... sometimes even a sweet gig, but that would entail another move, more massive life transitions, and starting all over. Also, I know enough now to know I may not always be stepping into a healthy environment. So I stayed. Now is this a permanent thing? Time will tell. But I planted my flag in Portland and decided that no matter what, I'm calling this place home. As a result, I've had to fully lean into this whole world of bi-vocationalism. And I'm glad I did. It changed my life.

Throughout this process, I realized it's not really that odd for me to do this. Sure, there's a part of the American workforce that certainly is transient. Then there's the other forty-to-fifty percent who don't move more than forty miles away from home. There are multiple storylines happening simultaneously. We have a migratory workforce and a stationary workforce. I also see this at play back home in Iowa.

My wife grew up on a farm. The farm has been in her family for generations. Both her parents farm but also work outside of the farm as it's relatively small. Throughout the many years I've known them, they've worked multiple jobs in various towns and cities. The constant factor for them is the farm. They are stationary. They're not uprooting every time an attractive job opportunity arises. So they stayed and took different jobs within their respective fields.

Pastor … church planter … missionary … if you feel called to a place, then why wouldn't you do the same? Too often ministry professionals are migratory like tech workers. Always on the move. When church planters move to a new city, they adamantly declare,

"God's called me here for life." And then after five years, your funds run out and all of a sudden you're barreling down the highway in a moving van onto your next ministry destination.

What if you stayed? What if, like a farmer, you're tied to your land? Your city? That you're staying no matter what? Funding runs out? No problem. Develop more income streams. I've now been in Portland long enough to see that most church planters don't make it past five years. *Most.*

PART-TIME

CHAPTER 4

SHAPING YOUR PATH

PASTORING

Of all of the times to be writing about developing a healthy part-time life! Yesterday was MLK Day. I (Sean) didn't have classes so in theory it was setting up to be a day off. In my mind all weekend I was formulating a plan to explore some obscure rural Oregon town.

The plan was to get up before dawn, grab my camera, and set off for central Oregon. There's an abandoned town I've been itching to explore. To walk around it, peer into buildings, and take photos. Since it's winter and dark by five o'clock, I figured I would be home well before then to enjoy the rest of the day and evening with my family.

But I never left Portland.

Instead, I worked from 8 AM until past 11 PM. I worked for five hours on an academic journal I co-lead, I led two online cohort calls, and then roasted coffee through dinner until I finished cleaning up at 11:15 PM. My trek across the high desert of central Oregon would have to wait. Was I wrong not to go? Is my life out of balance? Is there really such thing as balance?

Life is like a song. In our song each instrument represents one part of our lives. A responsibility. A job. The more we add the more complex the piece of music becomes. The result could be a beautiful masterpiece. But more likely what it means is that we have a lot of instruments that are out of tune and a performance in need to work.

The more we add, the more we need to keep all of these instruments in tune. Each additional instrument means more complexity. Therefore, what is needed is a growing ability and capacity to handle more stuff and do so with skill and precision so as not to fall flat or burn out. So what constitutes a healthy part-time path or life? Is there even such a thing?

This question actually came up in one of my cohort calls yesterday. The question was: how do you work hard, grind, or hustle and yet at the same time slow down? That seems paradoxical. Counterintuitive. But that gets to the heart of this chapter. In the midst of juggling everything or playing a multiplicity of instruments, how do you (a) do it well, (b) carve out margins, (c) be healthy emotionally, spiritually, socially, and physically, and (d) thrive?

The challenge before us is that there is no one-size-fits-all template. Andy is a pastor at Mission Church while leading Midtown Artisans. Oh, and he's a part-owner of a little store called MESA shop. I lead Intrepid, teach a full load in the university classroom, co-lead an academic journal, write, and run Loam Coffee. My time demands differ from Andy's. Much of my life is in sync with the rhythm of a school year. Andy's workload outside the church is project-oriented.

All of us are also wired so differently that one person's overwhelming schedule is another's normal week. Add to that different family dynamics based on the ages of our kids. The point? Finding and establishing a rhythm is unique to each person and oftentimes it takes experimenting to find the right balance. While I missed my big exploration day yesterday, the fact is I spent most of Sunday exploring new parts of Portland with my middle son.

PART-TIME

MID-BOOK PAUSE

REFLECTING ON THE JOURNEY SO FAR

PASTORING

Andy here with a mid-book pause. If you've made it this far with us, you're probably onboard with this part-time, bi-vocational thing. You've listened to our stories, decided you're not crazy, and considered that different paths exist. Before you trek on further with us, I'd like to invite you to assess YOUR potential path. Write in the book. You won't get much for it in trade at the bookstore anyway. ;-)

What is my vocational story, and how could it shape my path forward in ministry? What part-time potential can I see in my story?

If you could dream up a part-time ministry job, what would it look like? Where would it be?

If you could dream up a part-time job to accent your ministry work, what would it be? Imagine how it would fulfill the goals you have for ministry.

Do those dreams seem crazy? Why exactly? According to whom?

What unique opportunities for part-time ministry can I imagine having (connections, skills, hobbies, education, local opportunities)?

What are my unique roadblocks to part-time ministry (debt, family needs, personality type, other time constraints)?

What steps could you take to minimize your roadblocks to part-time ministry while maximizing opportunities?

If you could come up with one or two specific things to regularly pray about concerning these ideas … what would they be? When and with whom can you share these things?

PART-TIME

CHAPTER 5

WALKING WITH OTHERS WITH JESUS

PASTORING

The first job I (Andy) got that felt somewhat Christian was at the local Christian bookstore. They hired me on as a retail clerk. I was seventeen. It felt like a regular job, like the ones I'd been working since the day I turned sixteen. So far, I'd worked at good ol' Taco Bell (in the city that boasts some of the best Mexican Food in the US) and in the dining room of a retirement community. All the "real job" elements were there in the bookstore ... counting out the cash drawer, good customer service, profit margins, and marketing strategies, but it also felt like ministry alongside trusted friends.

One of my favorite roles was helping someone find their, or their friend's first, Bible. I loved to hear their needs try to help them find a Bible that fit just right. Some people needed one that they could read and understand. Some people needed one that matched the level of study they aspired to. Some people needed notes that would help them answer the questions about they were reading in Scripture. Still others needed something very practical like large print or a size they could fit in their glovebox.

On top of the biblical content of the job, there was a general mindset of ministry most of the time. Customers would share their struggles with us. We, as co-workers, would support and pray for each other. We invited one another to church and church events. We raised money for Christian causes. We learned from each other about all of the available resources for biblical and historical study. And then ... I got fired. I had a really hard time taking direction from the store's owners and blew it.

All of a sudden, I had to find a new job back out in "the world." That's when I went into car audio. The culture around car audio couldn't have been more different. The main goal was making money. Customers were often mocked. Salesmen and installers clashed. The guys took smoke breaks to relax from the stresses of life, and left work to get drinks before bed. A couple of coworkers went to church from time to time. Nobody prayed. Encouragement came in small doses. Discouragement came in waves.

The benefit for me was that it drove me deeper into my felt-need for my church, encouraging friends who followed Jesus, and time alone with God in the Word and prayer. Something about the Christian bookstore made me feel spiritually stable by osmosis. Something about being in the car audio bays made me feel spiritually starving. My presence in "the world" made me treasure my time with the church.

My journey since then has taken me back and forth between the feelings of being stable versus starving. I got my first church job after that job in car audio. After that job ran its course, I returned to car audio, but this time to an even more volatile work environment. I went off to a school in Chicago that broke me out of that cycle for a bit, and then returned to take on another ministry role with the Salvation Army. That role, however, did not leave me encouraged at all at the end of the day. I found myself constantly both spiritually and emotionally exhausted.

For the first time my ministry job didn't feel like it was helping me spiritually, something I would feel many more times in years to come. Fortunately, God reached down in an act of redeeming grace just at the right moment. I saw the owner of the bookstore, the one who fired me. I apologized to him for disrespecting him and not appreciating the job he'd given me back in high school. The whole exchange made me very nervous.

He looked me in the eye, with the greatest joy, threw his arms around me and cried out, "I was hoping you'd come back!" He offered me a job at his store again. In no time, he promoted me to store manager. Now I had to experience the store, that had once been my safe haven, as a leader. I saw the harder elements behind the environment of grace that the store had become. I had to hire and fire employees. I had to think more deeply about the business, without neglecting our mission of ministry. To do such things, I had to gain spiritual stability from outside of the store in order to create an environment in which my employees and customers could experience grace. For the first time I felt I needed both my church and the support of believing friends WHILE I was engaging in a marketplace job that focused on ministry. It wouldn't be the last.

Every week, when we who are ministers gather believers together for worship, we're inviting them to do exactly what I learned to do throughout those years. We are asking them to live their daily lives in their workplaces, homes, and surrounding culture as distinct followers of Jesus. We're asking them to spend their lives on mission, out and among people of "the world." We're asking them to value and press into their relationships with believers and the life of their local church. Our people need leaders who actually have lived, and I'd venture to say ... continue to live out that reality themselves.

Part-time pastoring can be a great method of building the kind of life our people can emulate and relate to. As our people struggle to integrate faith and life, so do we. As our people feel the need for Christian fellowship and encouragement, so do we. Unfortunately, many pastor-leader types are afraid they don't have time for, or are deluded enough to think that they themselves don't need, a supportive community of believers. But part-time pastors need them as much if not MORE.

Fortunately for me, despite my tendency toward self-sufficiency and self-reliance ... God led me to Rod and Josh.

When I first began the process of planting our little church out of our home-based small group, I began to look for some kind of organization to link up with. I looked at church planting networks and denominations that were active in the area. I stumbled on the Arizona Chapter of the Gospel Coalition. When I emailed them, I got Josh on the other end.

Josh was running a pastor's group in Phoenix and invited me in.

Though Phoenix is a bit of a drive, I decided it was worth it. Students I used to work with lived there, and I could find ways to make a day of the trip. I began to get to know the guys in the pastors' group, about 10 of them, and found them to be great comrades. In the years to come, these guys would invite my wife and me to marriage events, support our church with material resources, and, most importantly, become our friends.

Today I host a Gospel Coalition pastors' group in Tucson that brings together over thirty pastors who are getting to know each other better. I still feel connected to the guys in Phoenix too, and as I write these words I'm reminded that one of them is hosting me for a quiet weekend away at a property his family owns. I've never regretted the time taken to drive to or sit through these groups.

The Gospel Coalition may not be for everyone, but community with peers is essential. Some of the guys in our Tucson group overlook theological differences in order to foster these important relationships. I highly recommend that you find a group of people you don't lead or have to follow, that will walk with you and help you walk with Jesus. All Christians need accountability and encouraging relationships, and pastors aren't exempt. This is especially true for part-time pastors.

In my life, though, Rod has taken the relationship to an entirely different level. I think everyone in ministry needs a Rod. I met Rod at a church my family visited as we were in the planning stage of our church plant. Rod is a good thirty years my senior and has both failed and succeeded at planting a church. Although I was not in his denomination and stood to offer zero benefit to him personally, he decided to meet with me for breakfast after I met him. He and I have been meeting for breakfast every week for about six years now. He tells me his stories, listens to my ideas, tells me when I'm being an idiot, and encourages me when I'm afraid.

Recently, at a gathering of emerging church leaders, I was describing the ways Rod has met with me and our growing little team of church leaders. Rod used to feel like he was alone, like "a tree in a field." His ministry has become one of making sure that other young leaders aren't alone. One of the young leaders at the table exclaimed, "We need more trees!" He's absolutely right. Most of the pastors I know don't have a pastor. In Rod, I and a few of my friends, thankfully do.

I am really fortunate that God caused my path and Rod's to cross, and that Rod invited me to breakfast. Not all of our elders will be so confident. Some of them will need us to ask them for help. I would encourage you to do just that. If you don't have a "tree" already, go find one! Rod isn't great because he knows it all. Rod is just willing to be with us, and share his stories … some of them victories and some of them losses. If you think you don't have time to sit around and listen to someone else's stories, I want to challenge that assumption. Better to have whittled away the time than to walk alone through the trials and spiritual battles of ministry.

Through Rod, I got connected with some folks in his denomination (Christian Reformed) who are trying to help develop young leaders. One of the things that they've discovered is that young leaders often get themselves so deep into ministry and the busyness that comes with leading people that they begin to lose track of their own spiritual health. These young leaders forget to sit with Jesus in prayer. They stop reflecting and listening to the Holy Spirit. They get tired out, and become more susceptible to burn-out and temptation. They've decided that during this busy season in these young leaders' lives, they will strongly encourage them and even pay for them to take part in a silent retreat. The aim of the retreat is to give them space and rhythms over one week, which will offer them a pattern for the rest of their ministry.

Of course, I took them up on the offer. My fellow church leaders have been very attentive to my spiritual needs, and have mandated that I take a sabbatical at least every four years. When I signed up for the silent retreat, I was coming off of my sabbatical year, so I felt very much "in practice." A lot of the other guys seemed as if they needed time to settle into the idea of silence. For me, since I'd just taken a three-week trip alone with many long periods of silence, it was a welcome repeat of the wonderful time with God I'd recently experienced.

On the retreat, I wandered all around the Genesee Valley in Upstate New York. We took part in the rhythms of the Abbey of the Genesee, where Henri Nouwen had stayed when he wrote *The Genesee Diary*, which centered on singing the Psalms and prayer. I walked through the cornfields with geese flying overhead. I sat by rivers for hours at a time. I walked down railroad tracks and journaled on the deck of an old abandoned rail car. I memorized a Psalm. I prayed for hours. It was wonderful. As the sun rose on the last morning, I sang the doxology over a flock of geese as they awoke from their night's sleep, which is not something I typically feel free enough to do. I came back refreshed.

Doing ministry part-time can be taxing. Getting used to being in environments where you're stabilized and then spiritually starved can be tough to reconcile. Leading a ministry can often appear to be spiritually safe, but prove to be spiritually draining. Though part-timers might feel like they can't give time to such things as friendship and silence ... they need it more than anyone. Hopefully the people in your circles will see that and fight for you. If they don't, you'll have to advocate for it yourself. People need pastors and spiritual caregivers who are still receiving discipleship and walking with Jesus themselves.

PART-TIME

CHAPTER 6

PART-TIME PASTORING DISTRIBUTES THE MINISTRY

PASTORING

Sean here. For many, this notion of part-time pastoring or church planting along with other terms like bi-vocational or co-vocational seems to be fraught with tension. The fear or assumed reality is that this is a life lived at a frenetic pace ... maddening, consuming, and unhealthy in every way imaginable. But what if it wasn't?

Any career that we step into has all of these same realities. Whether you're a medical doctor, lawyer, startup entrepreneur, elementary school teacher, auto mechanic, or artist, there are inevitably seasons of a maddening workload and time constraints. The point is that this reality is not solely reserved for those stepping intentionally into part-time ministry. It's called work. It's called life. Welcome to adulting.

However, ministry is a unicorn when it comes to a job, a profession, a career, a vocation, or a calling. It was never meant to be a solo endeavor. We know from the New Testament that pastors, elders, and shepherds are to be focused on equipping the church to do the actual work of the ministry. Yet we still continue to have it all backwards. This is where it gets tricky when ministry is also your paid job because there's the tendency to assume then that since you're paid, it means … well, you're paid to *do* the ministry.

As a result, most church planters and pastors I know intentionally live frenetic lives. Many feel the crushing weight of cultural expectations whether from people in the church or from their denomination or network. To think of adding a part-time job or career outside of the church seems like a recipe for an early grave. But what if it didn't have to be that way?

What most ministry leaders never admit publicly ... let alone to themselves ... is that they carry with them almost a savior-complex. *They* are the ones called by God. As "God's ordained one," they assume they now have superhuman powers. But most full-time planters I know (and I mean *most*) spend a good chunk of their week doing stupid things ... hanging out on social media, recording podcasts, listening to many other podcasts, reading books, coffee appointments with other church planters and pastors, other networking meetings, and so on (OK, I admit this is hyperbole ... sort of). I could seriously trim off twenty hours a week from the activities of a church planter. Then what? If one really has all of that free time, then what? What does it mean?

It means that while we think we're "so busy," we're really not. That's why part-time pastoring is a good solution that erases all of the stupid things ministry people do during the week. It also removes from them their "savior" mindset and gives them instead the role of a distributor. That's actually a key analogy.

Too many pastors and church planters do ministry like James Harden (aka "The Beard") plays basketball. Most ministry leaders I know assume they are not only gifted but have the green light to do it all themselves. James Harden is a phenomenal player. I love watching him. Sure, he travels a lot with his step-back threes, but he's entertaining to watch. No one disputes that he's one of the most gifted offensive players we've ever seen in the NBA. I take nothing away from his talents and abilities.

But he's not much of a team player. He gets his own. He gets his shots off and the points. In some of his most prolific scoring nights, he would not even register an assist. You know … an assist. Where you actually pass the ball to your teammate and then *they* score a bucket. Nope, not The Beard. Ball movement (i.e., passing the ball around on offense) stops when it gets to him. Many church planters and pastors are like that. That's why we *need* part-time pastoring. You see, when you're doing it part-time you have to distribute the load. You can't do it all yourself.

Part-time pastoring or church planting gives you the green light to be a distributor and not the dude who keeps chucking up step-back threes. You're actually getting others involved, sharing the load, and playing the role of a catalyzer. Remember Ephesians 4? You know, we're called to equip the body to do the ministry and not do it all ourselves. Of course, this may hurt our image on social media because there just might fewer cool and hip photos of us preaching and leading out front. Somehow, we've turned ministry into a glamor show rather than the work of someone who simply trains, equips, serves, and delegates to others. But that doesn't fit into our CEO model of a pastor that we borrowed without much thought from the business world.

I believe that much of our frenetic life in ministry is because we've decided somewhere along the way that our primary role is to *do* ministry … and all of it. Besides, we tell people that God called *us* into "the ministry." As for everyone else? Well, their job is to tithe, show up (attendance is key), and work in the nursery since no church has ever successfully been able to staff their baby or toddler room. (Working with junior-high schoolers is a whole different animal). The gift of part-time pastoring or church planting is that since everyone knows that we cannot do it all ourselves, it becomes a team effort from the beginning. That is a healthy rhythm that benefits everyone. It also keeps the leader's ego in check.

The word I used in the previous paragraph is key ... "healthy." You can actually be involved in ministry *and* live a healthy life. It doesn't mean there's no drama, brokenness, pain, disappointment, frustration, betrayal, and so on. There is plenty of that not only in ministry as well as in life. The difference, though, is everything doesn't depend on the lone pastor or leader, because there are others to share the load with. Nor is your whole identity wrapped up in it. And anyway, we're all more than our titles.

In the previous chapter, Andy wrote about our own walk with Jesus as well as having others walk alongside us as we walk alongside others. This chapter addressed the obvious reality that there's only one Savior ... and we're not Jesus. When we accept that, we're free to love, free to serve, and free to train up and empower others to do the ministry. We're most effective when we do that as we maintain a life-giving relationship with Jesus. Part-time pastoring simply means that we have to because our time is limited. If anything, it forces us into a better rhythm and emphasis on distributing the ministry.

PART-TIME

CHAPTER 7

THE FUTURE IS PART-TIME

PASTORING

For me (Sean), living in a city like Portland is sometimes like living in the future. This is not true just for Portland, but for larger cities as a whole. Trends and fads usually begin in the bigger cities and emanate outward. There's usually a time gap before this wave hits smaller cities. Having now lived in Portland, and some years ago in Tucson where Andy is, I see at times the stark contrast between the two cities. It's not that one is better than the other, it's simply the way things go.

For example, I love coffee. The last number I heard was that Portland has well over seventy coffee roasters. My hunch is that it is actually higher. In comparison, Tucson has less than ten roasters ... easily. Sure, we could say it's a size difference, but Portland has 647,805 people and Tucson 535,677. Obviously when suburbs are added in, the gap only increases (Portland metro has 2.4 million and Tucson metro has 1 million). With that said, almost all of Portland's roasters are in the city and not the suburbs. We love our coffee, our breweries, and more.

Sometimes when I'm visiting a new city, my host will inevitably take me to (in their words) the "Portlandy" part of town ... usually a district or a few small blocks. What they have in a few blocks we have in a whole city. No, this is not cultural arrogance or anything like that. They're simply observations. However, when it comes to the future of church planting and why it is going part-time, I feel as if I'm afforded a front-row seat to watch where this movement and conversation is going.

I've been around Portland long enough now to see the typical church planting storyline. Church Planter A moves from Houston, Dallas, Nashville, or from a small town in the Midwest. Their denomination or network is desperate to get a foothold in Portland. Not just the metro area, but the city. Not just within the city limits, but the urban core. So Church Planter A, with his family in tow, lands in one of the trendy city center neighborhoods. Within months comes the horrific realization ... not only are there four-to-five other church planters in the neighborhood, but some of the most well-known and highly regarded "hipster" churches are also in their neighborhood.

The painful reality is Church Planter A is not nearly as cool as the pastor of the highly regarded hipster church. Any hope of snagging the low-hanging fruit of young adults looking for a church is gone. All of those people have already been swept up into a myriad of these hip churches. As a result, after three-to-five years, if Church Planter A had launched a worship gathering it is small, unassuming, and not the ticket to financial independence that he had hoped for.

Church Planter A then has a couple options: (A) stick it out and plead with donors for "one more year," (B) get a part-time job and settle in for the long-term, or (C) polish off their resume and look for a ministry gig elsewhere. OK, so what is the tension? I thought this chapter was about the future of part-time ministry, you say. Yes, yes, it is.

You see, there's an enormous difference between going in with the mindset where part-time church planting, pastoral ministries, or missionary work is the preferred future versus a desperate grab for a part-time job that you're not passionate about, not skilled in, and where the goal is to simply hold on until the church grows and can pay you full time. What we're talking about is the first option. That part-time ministry is the plan. It is the present and it is the future. Why is it the future?

I'd contend that much of church planting up until this point has been predicated on the church planter's ability to gather a group of unchurched or dechurched Christians. However, the explosion of church planting over the past few decades means that that demographic is no longer as available as before. They've mostly been accounted for. As a result, new church planters are forced (in a good way) to focus on people who do not have a church background and are not too keen to come to a weekend worship service. This gets to the heart of missionary church planting.

What that means is … church planters need a longer and longer runway to get airborne. If we're not focusing on unchurched Christians but instead those who're not predisposed to attending a worship gathering, then it'll take years for a church to form. But no worries. If the future is part-time planting, then we will have the patience and funding mechanism to see much fruit.

So what is your strategy?

If church planting doesn't quickly garner the financial support to sustain your livelihood, then how do you plan to stay rooted long term? It's this very conversation which has led me to the conviction and strong belief that by far the best church planters are locals. Indigenous. Whether they grew up in that town, city, state, or region, they are truly home. What does that have to do with part-time pastoring? Everything.

Why does it matter? How does it connect? Let's look at the familiar storyline of Church

Planter B to see the difference. Church Planter B feels burdened for their community. They know the people. They love the people. They have a history with the people. With a strong relational network in place, they venture out to plant a church. Maybe they previously were on staff at a church or came out of a campus ministry background. Sure enough, they're running hard in the church planting endeavor.

But like Church Planter A, they also face the reality that most of the accounted-for unchurched and dechurched have been swept up by other church plants. But Church Planter B knows this isn't a sprint. Besides, where do they need to rush off to? So their church bumps along. No, it didn't explode like they hoped. But part-time work or pastoring or planting is non-negotiable. It was built into their DNA from even before they began. Why? Because they're already home.

When Church Planter A runs into obstacles or barriers, there's always the option of "going home." But for Church Planter B, they already are home. In other words, they're already planning for the long-term. If that means working part-time, then it's a no-brainer. Maybe a component of this is to be focusing more on raising up and mobilizing church planters rather than constantly transplanting them from across the country.

Since more and more of the unchurched and dechurched are accounted for, planters … whether Church Planter A or Church Planter B … need a plan to stay for the long term. Part-time pastoring should be option A for most church planters and pastors.

I (Andy) can attest to what Sean is saying here. As the local guy who wanted to start a new church, I observed two key things. First, I have seen many transplants come and go. Transplants being church planters coming from elsewhere. Of course, there are exceptions! I have a few great friends in ministry who brought their fresh perspectives to Tucson, and have done well. Though I don't have data on this, my sense is that the planters that transplant often do especially well with existing believers who have also transplanted to the city and are looking for a new church. Most of these transplants have had to hustle and find outside income streams for themselves.

Second, I have seen that many church planting networks and denominations seem more motivated to "send" their people to places that need them, than they are to see someone leading in their hometown irrespective of their "brand" of church. If I'm anywhere near a correct assessment here ... then the planters who know their cities best, and love their cities the most, will need to find alternative ways to fund their lives of ministry. This tide seems to be changing, but there's a long way to go.

I have lived in Tucson as long as I can remember. I have lived and breathed Tucson air. I am well aware of the beautiful things that Tucson has to offer, as well as the pervasive darkness and brokenness that eats away at Tucson's soul. I have gone to church my whole life in Tucson. I've gone to churches that felt like remnants of a bygone era from a distant place. You know the little Pentecostal church you can find in just about every town? Or was it Baptist? Or Church of God? Yeah ... I went to some of those in Tucson. I also went to the big new church that swept in and gathered all the new suburbanites. I've been to the bilingual churches. I've been to several African American Churches. My family did the Tucson church tour, so when I think about what church should look like in Tucson, I have a clue. We designed our church plant with specific groups of local Tucsonans in mind.

I also have simply lived Tucson culture. I love to hear people describe Tucson to me. I've heard so many conflicting descriptions. One friend declared that Tucsonans all hide their true selves behind their garage doors. Others describe Tucson as a kind, liberal, and accepting city. Some say Tucson doesn't have racism like other cities. Some see Tucson's history as markedly racist, as the city has obliterated the vestiges of its truly original residents like the Tohono O'odham and the Yaqui.

I can't summarize Tucson myself. It's all those things in innumerable pockets. Ministry in Tucson has to look different depending on your street corner. I suppose it's kind of like that anywhere. The thing is, I have a lifetime of having stood at many of these street corners and watched. That's what best equips me to do ministry in this city.

The trouble I've found is that when you know a city well and want to do a targeted church plant that is in, of, and for your beloved city, you can't often gather other people's money for something so specific ... at least not at first. When you are planting the only church like the one you're planting, the concept isn't proven. People don't give to ideas as often or as much as they give to embodied movements. Also, such churches are likely going to be small. To dial in on a specific nook of community, they have to be more like boutiques than shopping malls. People and organizations aren't yet sold on small, and may never get there. Small communities will struggle to fund big ideas. Your commitment to a specific place you know and love must be coupled with your commitment to help provide the funding. You also may need to design a church that runs lean, and that's more than OK ... that's wise!

If you're reading a book like this, you're probably very committed to God, the gospel, and the church. You likely desire to see God's kingdom come, and for people to be reconciled to God and one another. Likely, you're also aware that much of Western Culture is "post-Christian," meaning that Christianity is and will be considered a relic of the past by most leading people in society. Going and gone are the days of faith communities having huge amounts of public support. Going and gone will be the days of behemoth church structures funded by the tithes and offerings of a majority of culturally dominant people. The tax incentives for ministry will likely disappear. So, are you still in?

The future will be different from the stories we've heard over the past hundred years. Our future churches will not come about the way our grandparents' or parents' churches came about. Some things will be more difficult. Some things will be more reasonable and simpler. We believe that one of the differences will be that the future of ministry will be part-time.

This is not necessarily a loss. We can be sad about this, or we can look for what God's doing. Maybe he's pushing us out of our church offices and denominational chat rooms and into the mission field. Maybe we're going to have a lot of fun, as we get to explore our vocational dexterity in ways that the old style of church didn't provide. Maybe God is creating an array of small and diverse churches that will reach the world with the gospel in incredibly effective ways. Whatever happens, many gospel carriers will have a side job. If we can wrap our minds around that, we can make it part of our strategy.

PART-TIME

CHAPTER 8

PART-TIME CAN BE FUN

PASTORING

Years ago, back when I (Andy) was a youth ministry leader, I set up a student leadership tradition in which we took our leaders to learn from diverse ministry professionals. One year we took them to visit a church planter in Seattle who was the son of one of our church's elders. Our goal was to learn from him about starting a church from scratch and to serve him in some way. We settled on making him a video, capturing his story in a way that would help his supporters to feel personally connected with him. It all sounded very fun to me. He seemed a little apprehensive.

Years later, reflecting on my journey of planting a church from scratch, I can understand why my new planter buddy wasn't as excited as I was. He was in the midst of launching a most difficult enterprise ... one in which you try to be a spiritual leader, while also offering something of a service to folks that they may or may not connect with. You're somewhere between being an event planner and a therapist ... but really doing the full job of both at half the pay and with deeper spiritual significance. I was now dropping a group of 15 kids into the middle of his life for a week, to whom he got to explain it all. We were serving him, I guess ... but we were also adding a ton of extra complex work onto his plate.

The trip went very well. The pastor and his team were actually very happy with the video we made for them, and we tried to stay out of his way as much as possible. We mainly filmed his church service, interviewed a few of his key leaders, and then hung out at cool Seattle coffee joints to edit the video. Some of us went to a ministry his church supported, and provided them some extra volunteer help. At the end of the trip, the pastor told me it had gone way better than he'd braced himself for. Our students learned a lot from him and his team, and enjoyed seeing a new city.

I got to stay at my new pastor friend's house during the trip along with a couple of my student leaders. I was taking notes, as I assumed I may be a part of a church plant someday. One morning I woke up a little early. I made a cup of coffee and heard a power saw running in the backyard. I casually filled my coffee cup and cracked open the back door.

The pastor was in the backyard constructing a fairly detailed cabinet of some kind. I watched him for a little bit, and when he took a break, I asked him if he found a lot of time to do handiwork around the house. He pointed to a number of outdoor furnishings he'd built. "I have to make time to build things," he said. "If I didn't do some work with my hands that I could actually finish, I'd go crazy." Over the years, those words have come back to me many times. Sometimes I feel like my "other job" has been a source of sanity and joy when ministry's been overwhelming.

Not every parallel job will be like mine, but my other roles provide me with a creative outlet that I have come to really appreciate. Whether it was actually building things, as I did in my earlier years, or brainstorming projects and processes with clients as I have done of late, my non-church work has been a source of great joy. I can hardly imagine what my life would be like, if the only creative work I was able to do had been what the church could provide. The church is and should be a very creative endeavor, but it is also a spiritual and complexly emotional endeavor. I've come to love the times I get to brainstorm or create something I can actually finish and be able to stand back and enjoy it.

Years ago, we got a call at Midtown Artisans about some office furniture a new studio needed. It sounded interesting over the phone, so we had the folks bring over their preliminary drawings. It was clear from the start that this was an ambitious operation. They needed a lot of furniture, and wanted it built and designed well to give a good impression. We even pitched them on our specialty concrete sinks and they seemed interested. When it was all written up, we were looking at the biggest job we'd ever bid out. We were still pretty unclear on what the studio really was.

Flash forward a few months and we were delivering the furniture to what was clearly going to be a very nice place. There were upstairs and downstairs offices, and two very spacious main rooms that we learned were for their filming. Flash forward another month … they invited us to the grand opening. They told us to bring along some business cards so we could get some exposure.

I've been to a number of these types of events, and I expected fifty people or so to show up. When we arrived, there were hundreds of people. There were local politicians and community leaders, there were clearly a bunch of people from out of town. A buddy of mine pointed out James Earl Jones' brother. We had no idea what a cool thing this was really turning out to be. This studio was a massive step for our city, as it provided LA-quality film production just a cheap flight away from Los Angeles.

The next month, they were filming an MTV reality show in the studio, and the executives were sitting around the conference tables we had made. Last I checked, Oprah was there and likely sat at a table we had made sipping coffee and washed her hands in one of our custom sinks. I remain extremely proud of the fact that my little company got to be a part of this project.

Not long after that big project a trendy young couple approached us about building a shelf and a point-of-sale stand for their store. It was a tiny job in comparison, but we get excited to build anything that people want built well. We were able to mount up their pieces just in time for their grand opening, and we love the little store they put together.

As the years have gone by, we've kept in touch with the co-business owners in our city and have been hosting little clearance sale parties with them. The most recent event felt like a who's who of local small business owners and their friends who came out for music, food, drinks, and deals. It was a warm gathering of people who deeply cared about each other, and there I was in the middle of it, as a local pastor. If not for this business, especially a business that initiated the event, I never would have been able to make these friends and be a part of this community that I deeply love and enjoy. These days, the local pastor usually isn't getting invited to the party, but the co-worker … the business owner … is.

I can't say that at this point that these business relationships have led to qualifiable spiritual results, but I'm OK with that. I will say that many of the folks I know through my business ventures have come the closest they've ever been to a Christian pastor through our relationship. From time to time I'll see some overlap between the two roles. Once, when a client was going through some relationship difficulties, I was able to enter into more of a pastoral role of listening to and advising them. Another time a guy I've worked with on many projects needed someone to go to divorce court with him, and I was the one he reached out to. We have a shared faith, but I am the only pastor he knows well enough to ask a favor like that.

If there's anything I've observed in all these years of ministry, it's that God works in people's lives and we are just a small part of the equation. Sometimes I selfishly like to think of myself as someone's hope, or worse … I fearfully see myself as their roadblock to seeing and trusting in Jesus because of my shortcomings. Usually though, when I remember accurately, I see that the people I've helped lead to Jesus have come to him through the work of God using a number of people in their lives. Sometimes there's the family member who shone a light into their family, or a friend who shared honestly with them about Jesus. I have a role, but I'm not the key player.

One guy at my church came to Jesus through the influence of an atheist podcaster. A Presbyterian pastor I once met told me a story of the best guy who'd ever come to be a part of his church. When asked why he came, he said it was because Joel Osteen recommended that every new Christian should find a local church … so he just went to the church with the sign down the street. In case you don't know …

most people don't usually connect Joel Osteen with the Presbyterians. My point is … we have no idea what our influence as a Christian out in the workplace, or at the work party, will have for the kingdom. Maybe you're just a "Joel" … pointing people to faith and the church that God's prepared for someone elsewhere. The immediate results that we can see aren't always of the highest importance.

The big idea is that we can and should enjoy the work we do when given the opportunity to work part-time outside of ministry. When we do, we'll be building the kind of relationships that we want the people of our churches to cultivate. The more fun we have with these roles, the more effectively we'll show our co-workers the beauty of God's kingdom. We should celebrate when our businesses win. We should celebrate the people we work with, and seek ways to spend meaningful time with them. We should do our shared work with all of our hearts, and so reflect the creator God who first displayed his glory to us in the work of his hands. All of this is kingdom building. All of this can be fun!

The longer I (Sean) teach and lead cohorts that help pastors, church planters, and missionaries launch businesses or non-profits, the larger the groundswell of momentum grows for this way of thinking and ministering. Yesterday I had two distinct (and typical) phone calls. One was from a businessman in rural North Carolina who wants to move to a small town in the Western United States to plant a church and open a coffee shop. The second phone call was from a campus pastor for a multi-site church who's ready to step away from the machinery of paid ministry to start a business so he can meet people where they're at and disciple them.

Interestingly, I had initially connected with this campus pastor about fifteen years ago when he was considering a move to Tucson to plant a church. At that time, I was a church planting strategist for a denomination there. After years of church planting thrills and sobering heartbreak, he's ready to love, serve, and minister in a new way. In other words, he called because he wants to process and dialogue about how to step into part-time pastoring. The vehicle to do so is to start a business or non-profit. Through our time together on the phone, I got the opportunity to share part of my own story.

The longer I do this and the more time I have here on earth, the easier it is to look back and see a connected thread through all of my adult life and ministry. But not just adult life. So many things were in the works long before I met Christ right out of high school. Predisposition, personality, and gifts have unintentionally pushed me forward on this trajectory that I'm on today. I wouldn't want it any other way.

In our cohorts I'm very up front with my own failures. I regularly tell cohort members that the reason why I'm doing what I'm doing in ministry and this wonderfully crazy world of bi-vocational ministry or part-time pastoring is simply because of my ineptitude in fundraising. Eighteen years ago, when I began my journey towards church planting, I was (and still am) a lousy fundraiser. As a result, within a couple of months of landing in Tucson to plant, I had no other choice than to strike out and get a job. But I had literally no idea what to even do. I've written in my other books about my journey and excursions into the world of living as a mountain biking guide while planting a church so I won't go into details here. However, it was that first step that changed my life. It was a branching point, a course correction, a Plan B that I had never foreseen.

Part of my journey and stories revolve around the worlds of church planting, academia, and startups. They make up my "tri-vocational" life. I wouldn't want it any other way. As a guide, when people learned I was also a pastor, I'd hear people recount stories of heartbreak and disappointment. In the classroom, more particularly after class, I've had students share with me gut-wrenching stories of pain and brokenness. But there are also fun stories and amazing times.

I've hiked and mountain biked with celebrities. I've had opportunities to teach and present to the entire faculty and staff during all-day trainings about understanding cities and Portland in particular. Even in the role of training church planters, I've had incredible experiences leading workshops with state university faculty, urban planners, architects and in fun places like breweries, on bike tours of cities, and coffee shops.

In the beginning of all this juggling, I almost had a sort of a bifurcation of my different worlds. There was my "ministry" world where I planted churches, trained church planters, and the like. Then there was my "secular" world where I led bike tours, taught university classes, or ran a coffee roasting company. I had always felt this tension. I was supposed to, right? There was "ministry" and then was "everything else" that was non-ministry ... or so I was taught.

And then one day, unintentionally, I forgot. It wasn't planned ... but that wall, that fictitious divide, that barrier simply disappeared. Gone. EVERYTHING was ministry. Literally the only difference was where my paycheck came from. That was it. All of a sudden I had a denomination kicking in part of my funding, two universities, and my coffee roasting company. That doesn't include other income streams like writing books, photography, graphic design, and more.

As I mentioned previously, now I'm more upfront to say that just as much, if not more, ministry happens in my "non-ministry" jobs. I have students stay after class in tears and share things such as about how their best friend just committed suicide, to recounting stories of childhood abuse, to struggling with life decisions, and so much more. It is an honor and privilege to listen, love, and pray for them in those moments.

Truth be told, I was never a good pastor or church planter. I'm not the most empathetic or compassionate person. But I've also realized that was and is a defense mechanism in pastoral ministries. Right? We get pummeled a lot. Whether we're a youth pastor always living in the senior pastor's dog house or as a church planter when people are livid that you teach and lead a certain way. I even recall one person early on in our church plant who met with me during the week because he had real issues with my teaching. He brought out his notebook and berated me for quoting non-Christian authors and then recounted how many times I used the words "I" or "me" in my teaching. Sure enough, his family left. I was relieved.

But outside of the ministry world, the whole narrative shifts. I am no longer on the defensive. I can simply be me (which sounds absolutely amazing to ponder). I'm not beholden to the template of what a pastor or church planter should or should not be. Instead, I get to ply my trades, get better at them, love freely, and look for those moments … those "God sparks" … when I sense the Holy Spirit is nudging and prompting people.

At the same time, it is precisely my bi- or tri-vocational life that opens up worlds of opportunities and conversations I never would have had before. A few years ago, while working on my PhD at Portland State, there were several instances in which classmates learned that I was a pastor and, while not even claiming to have faith themselves, shared struggles and asked me to pray for them. I had one professor recommend one of my books to some of the students.

For a stretch of time during my studies I worked for an urban sustainability pilot project on campus. Part of what we did through the university was to help and work with mid- to small-size cities to implement sustainability projects. My role was to coordinate with local universities and faculty to see if they could utilize some of their classes to conduct or help with research for these projects in their cities. We also worked with engineers, urban planners, and politicians in each city. As a result, we had numerous video calls with these leaders.

Since many of these projects were connected to a downtown revitalization project, inevitably the leaders were trying to connect with local organizations and institutions ... like churches. At one point during a video call, my supervisor, an avowed atheist and a former politician, nudged me and said, "Sean, you're a pastor, could you help these leaders connect with local churches in their cities?" That summer during our conference in Portland, I vividly remember riding our streetcar with some of these very same leaders talking about ways they could connect with local churches.

Part-time pastoring is FUN … very fun. What is interesting and needs to be pointed out is that I never had any of these ministry opportunities and conversations when all I did was full-time (paid) ministry. It wasn't until I stepped into part-time pastoring or church planting or ministry that these new worlds and spheres of ministry opened up in ways I never could have imagined before. This is the front edge, or frontier, of ministry. I never want to go back.

PART-TIME

CHAPTER 9

THERE WILL BE TRYING TIMES

PASTORING

It was there all along but I (Sean) didn't notice it. To say I didn't see it before wouldn't be true. Over the last couple of years as I read the New Testament every day I have set aside a different highlight color for any time and every place giving in the church was mentioned. We know the concept of tithing in the Old Testament did not carry over into the New. Instead what we find are numerous instances of churches gathering funds to help churches in other countries or cities that were going through famine or experiencing poverty. Funds, most of the time, were funneled to help believers in need. It is quite eye-opening.

What does this have to do with part-time pastoring or bi-vocational church planting?

Everything.

Paul the apostle ... the sent one ... has been our best example whether for missionary ventures, pioneer church planting, and so on. He's even our model for bi-vocational ministry. In fact, the term "tent-making" which we have used in the past to describe bi-vocational ministry comes from Paul's occupation as one who, well, made tents for a living. But yesterday morning I saw, working through 1 Corinthians, that Paul wrote something else that caught me by surprise. I was almost shocked and alarmed. It put a different spin on the whole conversation about bi-vocational church planting. Paul wrote, "To the present hour we hunger and thirst, we are poorly dressed and buffeted and homeless, and we labor, working with our own hands. When reviled, we bless; when persecuted, we endure" (1 Cor. 4:11-12).

While we cannot, nor should we, build a whole theology out of a passage extracted from one of Paul's letters, we can at least make some observations. Yes, we know Paul was bi-vocational. He made tents. We know at times he refused to accept any money from churches and instead worked his trade. Why? To show he wasn't in it for the money and because he didn't want to be a burden to the church. (Shhhh, don't share that passage with church planters … OK?)

What this passage reveals is that seemingly at times Paul's business wasn't that profitable. Was there a downturn in the economy? An over-saturation in the market for those also making tents? Did Paul land in a city that was experiencing population loss due to economic decline? We don't know.

But what we do know is this … his business wasn't affording him high-end sneakers, sweet threads, or a life of ministry luxury. He was hungry. Thirsty. At times homeless. He was poorly dressed. That last observation was ironically the most alarming to me. I thought, what church planter is poorly dressed? Have you been to Exponential? Most church planters seem to be style icons.

No, I'm not saying nice threads and style are wrong or anything like that. It just struck me that while we hold up Paul as the patron saint of bi-vocational ministry, we fail to take into account that maybe … possibly … it really wasn't as glamorous as we think it is (and I know that you already know that). He worked with his hands, plied his trade, and at times it simply wasn't enough. He went without. Without food. Without a home. In today's time and place he'd be on food stamps, maybe a recipient of Section 8 housing, shopped at Good Will, and was the beneficiary of the clothing bin at the local church's food pantry.

Is this what anyone imagines when we (myself included) extol the virtues of part-time pastoring? I've also have furthered the narrative that part-time ministry will fit seamlessly with church planting or pastoring, supply all of your needs AND desires, and more. It could. Or it could look and feel like Paul.

Paul's comment is a cautionary tale for us involved in ministry. Why are we in it? Career change? New job? A fun, cool, and hip church startup idea? Would we still do it if we experienced at least a fraction of what Paul went through? Hunger. Thirst. Housing scarcity. His low-wage job wasn't enough to cover rent, utilities, and food. Would we still plant? Sacrifice? Or would we simply pack up and find a cushie ministry job elsewhere where we can hang out at coffee shops more, blog, and spend more time on social media?

I know, I'm not being super nice right now. But these are the questions I ask myself first. You're simply getting to read my conversation with myself. Maybe what we're missing is this … a genuine love and brokenness for the people we long to see encounter the gospel. For that I think we'd give up almost everything. Do we love them? Long for them? Cry for them? Depending on how we answer that will gauge our willingness, like Paul, to be "poorly dressed and buffeted."

Sean and I had the discussion he just shared with you on a restaurant patio in Tucson on a nice sunny day. I agreed with him, and have experienced some of what Paul may have been referring to. Then again, I don't want to pretend like I've been in that bad of shape. Over the course of my whole part-time ministry journey I've been able to own a modest home, drive a decent (though high-mileage) vehicle, and support my thrift store shopping habit to some degree. I mean, I was hanging out with Sean on a restaurant patio ... and I hang out with people at a lot of coffee shops. I'm clearly not suffering that much.

That said, my family hasn't chosen the easy road by planting a very needed, but grassroots church. I am well aware that I would make a lot more money managing one of the thrift stores I shop at, than doing what I do today. That is a fact, by the way. A large thrift store down the street was looking for a new manager, and it paid double what I get paid by my church after seven years. We've made do so far, and we enjoy our lives! We've done so by renting a detached room of the home we bought ... and we bought the right house at the right time which saves us a lot of money compared to many of our friends. My wife also works a couple days a week as a nurse, which means we have great insurance and some extra income.

When we first planted our little church in our neighbor's yard, my wife and I had a serious conversation, which I believe was a critical step in our process. We thought we had about eight people committed to plant the church with us, and we knew that we were only interested in planting a church that reached out and cared for others. This meant that we couldn't in good conscience start off by budgeting a salary for me. We needed to prioritize generosity first, then ask God to provide from there. I remember discussing with my wife that it was possible that we'd never get paid by the church. We asked ourselves if we believed in starting a new type of church even if it never made us money. We ultimately decided we did, though we were nervous about what the future looked like, to say the least.

The little company I formed was my way to help contribute financially while still having enough flexible time to be a pastor. We had to lean on the little endeavor for a couple years, as the growth of the church was gradual.

Looking back, though, the money flow was only a minor part of the difficulty we faced which we never could have planned for or predicted.

I won't bore you too much with our troubles, but I will say that the enemy of our souls discouraged us amidst a number of trying circumstances in our early years of church planting. The lack of money only added a layer. An example would be the carbon monoxide leak we woke up to one Christmas Eve, which could have killed us, but instead just necessitated a complete replacement of our AC/heat system AND our home's gas lines. Our friends at church rallied to help us pay for the gas lines, and we got a no-interest loan for the HVAC system from a family member. It was very trying, but God provided in beautiful ways.

The darkest time for myself personally, so far, was when my dad died of cancer. I had no idea how deeply I would grieve his passing, and I wasn't expecting it. On top of that, our church was moving into a new building and I'd committed to overseeing renovations. On top of that … on my way to church one Sunday, a young guy rear-ended me and totaled the truck

I used every day for work and which I was in desperate need of during the church project. We were not only low on money, but I was low on just about everything I needed to get through the day. I was emotionally, spiritually, and physically exhausted.

Of course, in a community of Christians, we aren't just bearing our own burdens. Thankfully my friends were Jesus to me during those times, but sometimes they too needed Jesus to be made tangible. Early in our church plant, my company was just starting to take shape and I was collaborating with a friend who would eventually become my first employee and a leader in our church. We'd taken on what was for us at the time a huge project, and he and his wife were expecting triplets. It seemed like we were going to be able to finish the project before the due date, and so we were pushing hard.

Sadly, we never made it. They lost their triplets and spiraled into the chaos of suffering. This caught our whole community off-guard. We hadn't ever grieved with people like this. We honestly didn't know how to do it. On top of that, we all had our jobs and lives ... and for me, my job was with my grieving friend and our looming deadlines. I still look back at that time with deep sadness. I still feel that I was a mediocre pastor at best, as I tried to juggle the complexity of being a friend's pastor and supervisor at the same time. But God is faithful. They are still with us, as are their two sweet little boys that God gave them ... but the journey through that time was indescribably difficult. Being part-time didn't make that any easier at all.

The bi-vocational path doesn't guarantee that things will go well. I've heard friends get their hopes up that finding another job will keep the burden off their church, or provide their family with more money to support ministry. I'm sure that can be true, but it also presents new challenges. The truth is, there's no easy way. Ministry is bearing one another's burdens and letting people walk with you in your brokenness toward Jesus in the hope of kingdom come. Nothing about that last sentence is luxury. Part-time, full-time, or just being a Christian is by definition difficult, but good. It's why Jesus calls us to count the potential costs. All Christians count the costs and consider them worth paying, because Jesus paid far more out of love for us. Part-time pastoring won't be easy. Can you accept that?

PART-TIME

CHAPTER 10

PART-TIME ISN'T FOR ALL PEOPLE OR ALL TIMES

PASTORING

Thus far in this book I (Sean) have shared snippets of my own wrestling, stress, and feelings of inadequacy while juggling bi-vocational/tri-vocational ministry. The tension is always there. Stress can assault me out of the blue. Some weeks I am literally on fumes by the end of the weekend only to turn around and do it again. Last week was one such week.

I got back Sunday afternoon after being gone from Friday morning on a trip to Tennessee. I had been asked to consider joining the Board of Directors of a missions organization. Friday morning, I taught class and then went straight to the airport. By the time I got checked into my room that night it was 10 PM. The next day were meetings from sunup to sundown. Sunday morning was back on the plane for Portland. Got home and had to prep for classes for the week. My week was already full but then I roasted coffee Monday night from 5:30 to 11:15 PM, I taught a three-hour class Tuesday night, taught a four-hour class Wednesday night, roasted for four hours on Thursday night, and then served coffee at college basketball games Friday and Saturday night. Saturday and Sunday mornings were spent in prep time and grading.

By Sunday night I was spent.

Not every week is that way. But it does happen. However, like anything in life, the more we do something, the better we get at it. Interestingly just this morning, as I was journaling, I had a breakthrough moment of sorts. I wrote about how I'm finally hitting my stride with this lifestyle. In the midst of it, I've landed on several non-negotiables that keep me intact.

I work out and exercise five or six times a week. I get eight hours of sleep. I have my quiet/devotional times every morning (with a cup of coffee). I have a weekly lunch date with my wife. I read for fun.

It's taken a while to get to this place. For me it's an adventure. A thrill. A rush. I also don't want to make it sound like I'm going full throttle 24/7 because that is not true, but my average work week is probably 60 hours. Some weeks more and some weeks less. It's also seasonal. During school breaks when I'm not teaching it's even less. The point is that I've found my rhythm.

What I've also learned is that I've become pretty efficient. There's not a lot of fluff in my schedule. I get in, get my work done, and move on to the next project or job. Yesterday was typical ... up early for my quiet times. Social media posting for one of my jobs. Off to class to teach. Meet-up with a student after class to talk about his senior research paper. Back home to work on ministry stuff and, in this case, our newsletter. Lunch with my wife. Hour-long bike ride. Roasted coffee for two hours. Prepped for my evening class. A quick bite and then off for my four-hour class.

What may be typical for me could sound horrifying for others. We're wired differently. The point is for you not to emulate others but discover who you are, how God wired and gifted you, and lean into that more. There is no one-size-fits-all template in regard to part-time pastoring or church planting. Some may look at my schedule and lifestyle and get queasy. Others may shrug because it is already their lifestyle. Nor is this reserved solely for those in bi-vocational ministry.

Last night was the final evening of the intensive four-hour course I teach. It goes for five weeks. The program was designed for working adults. They enter into the program with an Associate degree, have class one night a week for two years, and they come out on the other side with their Bachelor's degree. The average age in the class last night was probably forty to forty-five years old.

I discovered on the first night of class that almost all of them work on average about three jobs. They have their main full-time gig which doesn't pay the bills. On the side they deliver food, work as a DJ, and many other jobs simply to make ends meet. On top of that they have families AND are going to school full-time. Although the class is five weeks long, we literally cram a traditional sixteen-week semester class into this timeframe. The reading and writing are intense.

You see, what we're talking about in terms of bi-vocational ministry is nothing new or even exclusively ministry-related. So many people are working at two, three or four jobs out of necessity. The question is … can you? Should you? Do you have the capacity? Do you even have the choice?

Andy here. As you've read this book you may have thought a couple things. Maybe you've thought, "I really relate to these guys." Maybe you love variety and starting things. Or … maybe you're thinking something along the lines of "I can't even manage juggling one job, laundry, and dishes without having a mental breakdown." I am the first to acknowledge that I am in a unique class of people. I love variety and being social. I love seeing a new thing start and then handing it off to someone else. I tend to have big ideas and a drive to go after them. And being a pastor I KNOW that is not everyone's bent.

The type of job combination you choose must be driven by an awareness of your capacities. For that matter, you ought to consider your capacity and personality as you ponder what types of ministry you move toward. Church planting is very entrepreneurial and also requires that the planter wear many hats. That type of person can usually manage another part-time job. Taking over an established church that's healthy and stable may not require the same variety of skill sets or personality traits. Taking over a small or declining church may require even more creativity or willingness to do multiple things.

I want to be clear that there isn't one path forward here. This is a process of assessing yourself and your God-given capacities. It's OK to look at other church leaders in your community and say … "I can't do what they do because I'm not them." That's just reality, and it's good. The church needs diverse leaders in every way, including diverse personality types and differing capacities. We still think you really need to consider the validity of part-time ministry, but be self-aware as you do so. Don't sign up for something you're not really able to pull off even with God's help.

It is also a good idea to recognize that your top priority is your personal health and wellbeing. Some part-time pastors think that they must work their regular J-O-B and then do everything a full-time pastor would. Never sign up for that! It's not fair, and it's not going to work. You still need days off and you still need sleep. If you are working two jobs, communicate to each of them that you have another priority. Your church needs to understand that you need more money and to rest, so you can't always be available when you're not working at the Wal-Mart or whatever.

Also, your Wal-Mart type job has to understand that you are committed to ministry from the outset. If someone in your church is dying, you need to prioritize that. You can't be the person who gets his shifts switched when you're committed to leading a small group or church service. Ultimately, you need to decide what's negotiable. If church is priority one by a long shot … communicate that. If providing for family is number one, your church needs to wrap their minds around that too. Believe me, it's better to talk about these things up front than to navigate the distinction in the midst of a crisis!

I have also observed in my journey, and in the journeys of my friends in ministry, that things change. Sometimes you start off part-time and your ministry needs you to devote more time at a later date. Sometimes you start off full-time and learn that adding a leader who's gifted in ways you aren't is more strategic than you having a full-time position. Sometimes one of your part-time gigs (ministry or otherwise) just needs to change. The latter has been true for me so far.

When I first started my church and the handyman company that morphed into my custom furniture shop, I was the main guy at both. I had my little truck full of tools and a backpack with my Bible and laptop, and I was like a traveling one-man band careening through the city. I'd knock out some bookshelves, grab a quick lunch and talk about church with somebody, kick out a paragraph or two of my sermon and send a church email, and then log my receipts for everything before I went home. It was all on me, but I decided exactly what to take on in each realm. It was tough and lonely in a way, but simple and customizable in ways I didn't even realize.

As time went on both entities became inhabited by other people. I hired employees to help me at the shop and we took on more clients. The church grew a bit, and we started to have some other part-time staff members. It took a little too long for me to realize it, but I was still functioning like I did when I started. I generally knew what I wanted to see happen, and I just took care of my tasks toward those goals expecting the newly involved people to do the same.

Finally, it became apparent that what the people who worked with and for me needed was my leadership, not my ability to complete tasks. It was better for me to have them build the shelf, send the email, and in some cases write the sermon, in order that I could set aside time to think, plan, and lead.

Honestly, I'm still working on that transition. It almost feels wrong, though I know it isn't. I keep plenty busy taking care of big-picture questions, meeting with key leaders, and learning how to lead out of my strengths on top of preparing to preach and discipling a few people in our church. My time split has changed pretty dramatically. My business used to get at least fifty percent of my week, if not more, but now I usually give it about ten hours. I have some great people in place who fulfill the needed roles far better than I did. Our craftsmanship is better in their hands. The day-to-day management is better too, especially as it became a far more demanding task. Part-time today looks different for me than it did a year ago. By the time you read this, I predict it will have changed again.

Though I am in my late thirties as I write this book, I have also walked alongside older friends in ministry. Something I've noticed is that some of them started off part-time and then moved to full-time. A good friend of mine owns a local book store and transitioned into being a church elder and then a pastor. Now he's full-time at the church and can hardly handle the load sometimes. But I've also see that as ministry leaders age, they sometimes need to return to being part-time. Sometimes this is because their ministry ages with them and has to be downsized. Sometimes this is because some tasks are best placed in new leaders' hands, and the older leader enters into something like a pastor/consulting role. Things change. If you're full time now, as I once was, you may not always be. If you're part-time now, you may need to go full-time for a while.

I currently work with a pastoral apprentice at our church. In some ways I see a lot of myself in him. In other ways we're very different. As he tries to work out his game plan for life and ministry, I wonder what it will look like for him. I can see ways in which roles outside of the church may be a good fit for him, and could really keep him grounded in the needs of his city and its people. On the other hand, I can see that his capacities are different than mine. One is the capacity for risk.

I don't love risk, and certain risks worry me more than others, but I have noticed that I can move forward into something that's unsure with a certain level of comfort. He operates differently. He is very creative and can think on his feet in ways I can't, but he may not jump at the same opportunities I would. He's a great apprentice to me, because he's different from me. Maybe this means that he leads as a part of a team that balances him out and keeps one foot in another role. Perhaps it means that he needs to be in a more established environment, such as the one I helped build that brought him in. Whatever the case, he won't always be my apprentice and I can guarantee his method of ministry won't look exactly like mine.

As you move forward into whatever stage God has for you next, I encourage you to remember that there isn't one mold you need to conform to here. Even Sean and I have very different lives. Through trial and error, we've figured out our own unique rhythms for work and rest. We've learned what our capacities are, and which roles can best help us minister, make a living, and be who God created us to be in the world of work. You will find yours. It will take time, reflection, and re-grouping, but that's OK … that's normal.

PART-TIME

CHAPTER 11

JESUS, WITH US ALWAYS

PASTORING

Roots and foundations are fascinating to me (Sean). I'm always interested in the "why" questions. Not simply "why" but the story of how things came into being. That's why I love history and in particular urban history.

Our dual locations, Andy in Tucson and me here in Portland, make me mindful of roots, foundations, and history. It was in Tucson that I first developed a love for cities. It was also where I simultaneously found my love for urban history. You see, for years working as a hiking and mountain biking biking guide, I spent a lot of time in the desert. It was there I uncovered or found a history that was just beneath my feet.

From pottery shards to foundation stones of pit houses and walls to mortars and pestles, I literally stumbled upon the remains of a culture and civilization that vanished nearly 600 years ago. Running my fingers over countless pottery shards sent me on a quest and an adventure to learn more. Along the way I encountered other figures from Tucson's past ranging from the Hohokam, Father Kino, early Spanish and then Mexican miners, Apaches, and so many more. It is a rich and colorful past that drew me deeper into its history.

What keeps us rooted? What keeps us grounded? What keeps us anchored in the frenetic world of part-time pastoring or church planting? The answer is a vibrant walk with Jesus.

The older I get the more I see all around me the carnage of life's decisions. I vividly recall at a men's retreat in college when one of the speakers made an almost prophetic announcement, "Look around, within ten years only a couple of you will be walking with

Jesus." We all squirmed. "Surely it won't be me," we probably thought to ourselves. We were all ministry-minded people. But he was right.

In the world of "professional" ministry, most pastors or church planters I know end up leaving ministry altogether. Obviously that last statement is fraught with tension. Who says ministry needs to be a career and the source of one's livelihood? Hopefully by now you know that's not what I'm saying. Instead, most have moved on from any involvement in ministry. They hopped the tracks of their career path and are onto something else. They may or may not even be involved in a local church.

What happened?

The same thing that could happen to you … or to me. Again, let me reiterate that I'm not saying that "real" ministry happens only as long as someone is paid to do it. I don't even assume one needs to receive any money to do ministry. But what I am saying is that somewhere along the way, whether from deep hurt (which most often is the case), or from burnout, or some kind of self-implosion, they've walked away from both their ministry and their faith.

So how do we stand our ground?

Due to the complexity and the juggling that part-time pastoring demands, there's even more of an impetus to deepen our walk with Jesus. Cliche? You bet. Accurate? Spot on.

To be honest, I'm currently in a phase where I'm licking my own wounds. More than anything it was a realization that after a couple of decades of riding this wild unbroken horse called ministry that I was myself carrying some scars. I was running hard for so long I didn't attend to my own needs and the hurts continued to mount. These hurts and wounds are not common to only ministry, but you know the list ... betrayal, friendly fire, unjust actions by those in authority over you, and then there's the whole odd dynamic of how competitive and performance-based ministry can be.

Maybe it is because I've been involved in church planting now for about twenty years that I see this narrative played out over and over again. Competition and performance-driven ministry leave so much carnage, so many broken lives and marriages along its well-worn path. Just this week I heard of another church planting acquaintance of mine who has to step away from his brand new (yes, brand new) church plant. Why? Because his marriage is crumbling. This story is merely representative.

Another church planting acquaintance also landed in his city with so much fanfare that "success" was inevitable. He had all the hype, the style, the social network, the connections, and the energy to not only plant a church, but to do so with massive explosive growth. And in one of the most unchurched parts of the country. Sure enough, launch Sunday came and went and it happened. Explosive growth. Hundreds gathered. Their Instagram page was as good as it gets. There was a flurry of activity. Then something broke. Literally. His mental health. He was found wandering the downtown streets confused. He had to step away.

I wish I could say these stories are atypical. Instead these are much more normative than we'd like to admit. Much more than your denominational leader will let on. That's because their livelihood is also tied to how many churches get planted, leaving them no other choice to play along and push for more and more church planters. Assessments aren't the cure-all. They don't reveal much other than some Type A competencies. Since church planting has devolved into techniques, competition, branding, marketing, and being overtly performance-driven, it is no wonder why a leader's health, marriage, and walk with God crumble.

Reflecting on what the speaker said to our group in college and now looking back over my twenty-plus years in the ministry world, I can see that what keeps us grounded or rooted has nothing to do with technique or skill. It has everything with a dynamic relationship with the living God. That doesn't mean we won't go through many dark nights. Sometimes as we're wracked with pain, all we cling to is trust that God is with us even when we cannot sense his presence. I am also comforted that many biblical figures also went through this.

In my morning quiet times, I've been reading through the story of Joseph in Genesis.

As always, every time reading the Bible I catch new glimpses. Perspectives I never saw before nor considered. Since we know how each story or narrative ends, it is easy to simply read it again without much second thought. But this time through had me reflecting on what Joseph was seeing and experiencing. How many painful years did he suffer through from the time he was sold into slavery as a youth to when he was elevated to rule over Egypt? We're not privy to most of his thoughts whether from the pit into which his brothers threw him, to being sold into slavery, to working for Potiphar and being falsely accused by Potiphar's wife, to imprisonment, and so on. What we do know is that when he finally confronted his brothers face to face, his heart was tender and he rushed to forgive them. Only a softened heart could ever do such a feat. God was his constant anchor.

How do we do the same? What does that look like? To keep rooted in Christ and at the same time let him be our anchor. Those might sound like cliches, but they're what is needed.

Just the other day, I (Andy) had one of those moments. You could call it a bit of a breakdown. Or I just lost my handle on things for an hour. Discouragement set in. It felt like I have worked so hard for so long … and for what? Is the kingdom growing due to all my work? Am I bringing about the restoration of people's lives and our community? It felt like I was making very little progress. I was plowing so hard just to yield enough produce to survive. Have you ever felt like that?

Most of us have. If you haven't yet … you probably will.

Is it OK to feel these things?

I think we need to feel this way from time to time. Because it brings up the question … Why am I doing this? What is this all about?

I answered that question years ago when I considered whether or not I'd be a pastor whether paid or not. I felt a call. It was not a call to ministry per se. No, it was a deeper call. It was a call to follow Jesus. It was a call to do things WITH Jesus that he was already doing in our world and for his kingdom. It was a call to build his church, which means it was a call to walk with Jesus alongside the people who make up his body, his physical representation here on earth. Ultimately, it was a call to live with Jesus, no matter how I was to divvy up my time.

When you hit walls in ministry, Jesus responds by asking again the question, "Do you love me? Do you really? Do you deeply and unconditionally love me?" And you're invited to answer. You aren't yet answering a call. No, you are answering a personal question from a personal God who promised to walk with you. And you have to re-examine it all. Why am I doing this? Do I love Jesus? Do I know him well anymore? Do I care? And then you answer. We, like we read about the Apostle Peter in John twenty-one, should have this dialogue with Jesus.

I'm so grateful for God's sustaining grace, as shown in this most recent instance, through the ministry of my wife. She looked at me and said, "You know you want to do this." She was right. Why? Because it was never supposed to be about results and productivity, but about walking with Jesus. And I said, as I hope I will keeping saying in the future, "I know … and I do." "I do want to do this. I do love you, Jesus." And then you hear the inner voice of Christ whispering, "OK. Feed my sheep." "Feed my stray, difficult little lambs." The call to ministry. First love, then ministry.

Look, ministry is hard. Full-time or part-time, ministry is hard stuff. The minister is often expected to be an organizational leader, a delegator, a counselor, and a teacher. It's really too much to ask. In a way, it's the impossible task. Look at Jesus! How well did his ministry work here on earth? He built a following, and lost it. Everyone loved his teaching until they didn't. Sometimes even his miracles were at best forgotten, and at worst considered demonic. If anyone can understand that saving people's lives can kill you, it'd be Jesus. And maybe that's exactly the point.

Jesus, of course, told his disciples that they'd experience the same rejection and opposition that he did (John 15:18-16:4). He never painted the job of being a Christian, let alone a leader, as being easy. He told them they'd have trouble (John 16:32-33). Through them, he was also telling us! So what kind of solace does he give us? Primarily two things. First, he gives us the assurance that after all is said and done, that he has already overcome the oppositional forces we face. He promises us ultimate victory, even though we may not see it in this life. And second, he promises that he will never leave us (Joshua 1:5 and Hebrews 13). He promises to be WITH us always (Matthew 28:16-20).

What we discover in all of this, is that Jesus knows us deeply and wants to walk with us as we await by faith his ultimate victory. Since failure isn't on the table, we can rest in his accomplishment as we seek to fulfill his great commission to the church. Since he has experienced acutely the pain of ministering in a broken word, he is the most compassionate companion on the journey we will ever need. Our experiences of the trials of ministry, as well as the victories, are opportunities to know Jesus more. They are pathways to relating to the only sufficient minister the church will ever have.

The only way to live the Christian life as intended, is to see it as a lifestyle that places us relationally close to Jesus. He smiles when we succeed … "Well done, good and faithful servant!" He weeps with us when we're confronted with pain and death. He feels the sting when we're rejected and maligned. He feels the disappointment when we pour out our souls and nothing seems to change. No … we are NOT alone. We are with our Lord, our God, our Elder Brother, our Friend, our Pastor.

Whatever you do, part-time or full-time, do it with Jesus. Stay connected. Learn to recognize him as he walks the road with you. Talk to him constantly throughout the day, before meetings, mid-meeting, when someone's running late! Read his word to become familiar with his voice. When you hear internal (or external) berating … force those words to square with the words Jesus said to those he loved and called. Renounce those accusations when they fail the test. Learn to hear his graceful reminders … that he is with you. Imagine God as the father with arms wide open waiting to embrace the prodigal son he loves. When you fail, RUN TO HIM! Confess your sins. He loves to redeem and restore YOU, not just the people you're supposed to be reaching.

And what about those people you're supposed to be reaching? What do they need? Do they need your perfect sermon or your professional ministry? Oh no! They need the same Jesus you need. And the human leader they need, is one who is learning to love and follow Jesus. If you are doing that, you WILL shepherd them well. They will follow you as you try to follow Jesus.

We have one hope of glory. It is Jesus Christ in us. Whatever strategy you employ … however many hours you devote, this is our hope. If you try ministry and it doesn't work out and you instead become a full-time non-pastor, that is OK. In fact, maybe that's perfect. Maybe that is where Jesus will lead you, so that you can know him more. Maybe God will give you a bunch of his sheep to lead, which turns out not to be easy at all. In that place too, you will need one thing. Jesus Christ, the hope of glory … our brother, our friend … our pastor.

PART-TIME

ABOUT

THE AUTHORS

PASTORING

Andy Littleton has been in some form of ministry since age 18, but has always dabbled in other vocational endeavors. In 2014 Andy planted what would one day merge with another small church and become Mission Church in Tucson, AZ with the help of his wife, daughter, and a small but amazing group of friends. Throughout that journey Andy founded a small handyman company, Midtown Artisans (a custom furniture shop), and MESA shop (a local and online retail store). He also has served on several non-profit boards and as a Mission Network Developer for Resonate Global Mission.

Sean Benesh lives in the Pacific Northwest and is a professor, author, and leads an initiative called Intrepid. He is the author of *Through Barren Wastelands* and over a dozen other books related to church planting and the city. www.seanbenesh.com

Made in the USA
Las Vegas, NV
17 November 2020

11060698R00115